ReasonML Quick S...

Build fast and type-safe React applications that leverage the JavaScript and OCaml ecosystems

Raphael Rafatpanah
Bruno Joseph D'mello

Pack<t>

BIRMINGHAM - MUMBAI

ReasonML Quick Start Guide

Copyright © 2019 Packt Publishing

All rights reserved. No part of this book may be reproduced, stored in a retrieval system, or transmitted in any form or by any means, without the prior written permission of the publisher, except in the case of brief quotations embedded in critical articles or reviews.

Every effort has been made in the preparation of this book to ensure the accuracy of the information presented. However, the information contained in this book is sold without warranty, either express or implied. Neither the authors, nor Packt Publishing or its dealers and distributors, will be held liable for any damages caused or alleged to have been caused directly or indirectly by this book.

Packt Publishing has endeavored to provide trademark information about all of the companies and products mentioned in this book by the appropriate use of capitals. However, Packt Publishing cannot guarantee the accuracy of this information.

Commissioning Editor: Richa Tripathi
Acquisition Editor: Noyonika Das
Content Development Editor: Mohammed Yusuf Imaratwale
Technical Editor: Sachin Sunilkumar
Copy Editor: Safis Editing
Project Coordinator: Kinjal Bari
Proofreader: Safis Editing
Indexer: Tejal Daruwale Soni
Graphics: Alishon Mendonsa
Production Coordinator: Nilesh Mohite

First published: February 2019

Production reference: 1280219

Published by Packt Publishing Ltd.
Livery Place
35 Livery Street
Birmingham
B3 2PB, UK.

ISBN 978-1-78934-078-5

www.packtpub.com

Mapt

mapt.io

Mapt is an online digital library that gives you full access to over 5,000 books and videos, as well as industry leading tools to help you plan your personal development and advance your career. For more information, please visit our website.

Why subscribe?

- Spend less time learning and more time coding with practical eBooks and Videos from over 4,000 industry professionals

- Improve your learning with Skill Plans built especially for you

- Get a free eBook or video every month

- Mapt is fully searchable

- Copy and paste, print, and bookmark content

Packt.com

Did you know that Packt offers eBook versions of every book published, with PDF and ePub files available? You can upgrade to the eBook version at www.packt.com and as a print book customer, you are entitled to a discount on the eBook copy. Get in touch with us at customercare@packtpub.com for more details.

At www.packt.com, you can also read a collection of free technical articles, sign up for a range of free newsletters, and receive exclusive discounts and offers on Packt books and eBooks.

Contributors

About the authors

Raphael Rafatpanah is a husband and father who wonders how he's going to pique his three-year-old daughter's interest in programming. With a background in business and math, he got started writing software to automate the data entry process at his family's business. Now, he's passionate about frontend development and the web platform. In his spare time, you'll find him searching for excellent sushi, photographing the world, and working on the elusive side project.

> *I'd like to thank my wife, **Amy**, for embarking on this journey with me, even when she was concerned that our daughter's first word would be "JSON", and for not slapping me when I responded with "it's still data."*
>
> *To my daughter, **Zoe**, you're such a joy and I'm so proud of you. Your smile warms my heart.*

Bruno Joseph D'mello is proactively working at Truckx as a full stack developer. He is a JavaScript enthusiast and loves working with open source communities. He possesses more than 6 years' experience in web development. Bruno follows kaizen and enjoys the freedom of architecting new things at work. He is socially active via coaching in web technologies and participating in other research projects and meetups.

When not engaged with technology, Bruno likes to spend quality time traveling with family and friends.

> *I would like to thank my family for their patience and support, especially my mom.*

About the reviewer

Adam Coll is a full stack web developer and probably will be tomorrow. He has been at it for 10 years and loves the ever-changing and fast-paced landscape that is the web platform. Right now he's either fixing bad code he wrote last month, thinking about bad code he wrote yesterday or writing code that he doesn't realize is bad yet.

Packt is searching for authors like you

If you're interested in becoming an author for Packt, please visit `authors.packtpub.com` and apply today. We have worked with thousands of developers and tech professionals, just like you, to help them share their insight with the global tech community. You can make a general application, apply for a specific hot topic that we are recruiting an author for, or submit your own idea.

Table of Contents

Preface — 1

Chapter 1: Introduction to ReasonML — 5
  What is ReasonML? — 6
  Why Reason? — 8
    Support for immutability and purity — 8
    Module system — 11
    Type system — 11
    Cross-platform — 11
    Maintainability — 12
    Interoperability — 12
    ES2030 — 12
    Community — 13
    The Future of ReactJS — 13
  Exploring Reason — 14
    Data structures and types — 16
      Creating our own types — 16
      Pattern matching — 17
    Making Invalid States Impossible — 23
  Summary — 24

Chapter 2: Setting Up a Development Environment — 25
  The Reason toolchain — 26
    Installing BuckleScript — 26
    Editor configuration — 26
  Setting up a pure Reason project — 27
    The bsconfig.json file — 29
      The warnings field — 31
      The package-specs field — 31
      The suffix field — 32
      The sources field — 32
    Working with DOM — 32
  Setting up a ReasonReact project — 34
    Improving the developer experience — 35
  Summary — 37

Chapter 3: Creating ReasonReact Components — 39
  Component creation basics — 40
    Component templates — 41
    self — 42
    Event handlers — 42

Table of Contents

unit	42
JSX	43
Props	44
Children	45
Life cycles	47
Subscriptions helper	48
Stateful components	**48**
State, action, and reducer	49
Refactoring	51
Instance variables	55
Ref and mutable records	55
Navigation menu	**57**
Bindings	59
Events	60
Js.t Object	61
Adding actions	61
Inline styles	64
React ref	66
Velocity	66
Client-side routing	**68**
Current route	70
Helper functions	71
Usage	72
Summary	**73**
Chapter 4: BuckleScript, Belt, and Interoperability	**75**
Module scope	**75**
Data structures	**77**
Array	77
Using the Reason standard library	78
Using the Belt standard library	79
Using BuckleScript's built-in JavaScript bindings	79
Using a custom binding	79
Using raw JavaScript	80
List	81
Recursion	82
Pipe operators	**84**
Using Belt	**85**
Option module	85
List module	86
make	86
makeBy	87
shuffle	87
take	87
Deck of cards example	88
Currying	89

[ii]

Uncurried functions	90
makeByU	91
JavaScript interoperability	92
Using JavaScript in Reason	92
Understanding the [@bs.val] decorator	92
Understanding the [@bs.scope] decorator	93
Understanding the [@bs.send] decorator	93
Understanding the [@bs.module] decorator	94
Reasonable APIs	94
BuckleScript documentation	95
Binding to existing ReactJS components	96
Importing dependencies	96
Creating the make functions	97
Using [@bs.deriving abstract]	97
Using the components	98
Summary	100
Chapter 5: Effective ML	101
Module signatures	102
Module types	103
Abstract types	103
Using module signatures	104
Phantom types	109
Polymorphic variants	112
Would this work with normal variants?	113
Advanced type system features	114
Summary	115
Chapter 6: CSS-in-JS (in Reason)	117
What is CSS-in-JS?	117
A brief history	118
Using styled-components	118
Using [@bs.variadic]	120
Using bs-css	122
Trade-offs	126
Other libraries	126
Summary	127
Chapter 7: JSON in Reason	129
Building views	130
File structure	130
Updating the router and navigation menu	130
CustomerType.re	131
CustomerList.re	132
Customer.re	133
Integrating with localStorage	137

Populating localStorage	137
DataPureReason.re	137
Validating JSON strings	138
Using Js.Json.classify	138
Writing to localStorage	142
Using bs-json	**144**
Using GraphQL	**146**
What is GraphQL?	147
When using GraphQL, do I need to create JSON decoders?	148
Summary	**148**
Chapter 8: Unit Testing in Reason	**149**
Testing with Jest	**150**
Installation	150
Our first test	151
Testing business logic	154
Reflecting	159
Summary	**159**
Other Books You May Enjoy	**161**
Index	**165**

Preface

ReactJS has changed the world of frontend development as we know it. Its creator, Jordan Walke, also created ReasonML and ReasonReact as the future of React. React's abstraction of the DOM allows for powerful programming paradigms that help solve JavaScript's maintainability problem, and in this book, we dive into exactly how Reason can help you build simpler, more maintainable React applications. This book is a hands-on guide to building React applications with ReasonML.

Who this book is for

The target audience of this book is JavaScript developers who are familiar with ReactJS. No previous experience with statically typed languages is required.

What this book covers

Chapter 1, *Introduction to ReasonML*, discusses the current state of web development and why we would consider ReasonML for frontend development (and more).

Chapter 2, *Setting Up a Development Environment*, gets us up and running.

Chapter 3, *Creating ReasonReact Components*, demonstrates how to create React components with ReasonML and ReasonReact. Here, we begin building an app shell that we add to throughout the rest of the book.

Chapter 4, *BuckleScript, Belt, and Interoperability*, gives us a well-rounded understanding of Reason's ecosystem and standard library.

Chapter 5, *Effective ML*, dives into some more advanced features of Reason's type system using business examples.

Chapter 6, *CSS-in-JS (in Reason)*, shows how CSS-in-JS works in Reason and how the type system can help.

Chapter 7, *JSON in Reason*, demonstrates how to convert JSON into data structures in Reason and illustrates how GraphQL can help.

Chapter 8, *Unit Testing with Jest*, jumps into testing with the popular Jest testing library.

To get the most out of this book

You should be familiar with the following:

- The command line interface
- GitHub and Git
- A text editor such as Visual Studio Code

Download the example code files

You can download the example code files for this book from your account at www.packt.com. If you purchased this book elsewhere, you can visit www.packt.com/support and register to have the files emailed directly to you.

You can download the code files by following these steps:

1. Log in or register at www.packt.com.
2. Select the **SUPPORT** tab.
3. Click on **Code Downloads & Errata**.
4. Enter the name of the book in the **Search** box and follow the onscreen instructions.

Once the file is downloaded, please make sure that you unzip or extract the folder using the latest version of:

- WinRAR/7-Zip for Windows
- Zipeg/iZip/UnRarX for Mac
- 7-Zip/PeaZip for Linux

The code bundle for the book is also hosted on GitHub at https://github.com/PacktPublishing/ReasonML-Quick-Start-Guide. In case there's an update to the code, it will be updated on the existing GitHub repository.

We also have other code bundles from our rich catalog of books and videos available at https://github.com/PacktPublishing/. Check them out!

Conventions used

There are a number of text conventions used throughout this book.

`CodeInText`: Indicates code words in text, folder names, filenames, file extensions, pathnames and variable names. Here is an example: "Run `npm run build` to compile `Demo.re` to JavaScript."

A block of code is set as follows:

```
"warnings": {
  "error": "A"
},
```

When we wish to draw your attention to a particular part of a code block, the relevant lines or items are set in bold:

```
/* bsconfig.json */
...
"sources": {
  "dir": "src",
  "subdirs": true
},
...
```

Any command-line input or output is written as follows:

```
bsb -init my-reason-react-app -theme react
cd my-reason-react-app
```

Bold: Indicates a new term, an important word, or words that you see onscreen. For example, words in menus or dialog boxes appear in the text like this. Here is an example: "The type of padLeft is (string, some_variant) => string, where some_variant uses an advanced type system feature called **polymorphic variant** that uses [@bs.unwrap] to get converted to something JavaScript can understand."

> Warnings or important notes appear like this.

> Tips and tricks appear like this.

Get in touch

Feedback from our readers is always welcome.

General feedback: If you have questions about any aspect of this book, mention the book title in the subject of your message and email us at `customercare@packtpub.com`.

Errata: Although we have taken every care to ensure the accuracy of our content, mistakes do happen. If you have found a mistake in this book, we would be grateful if you would report this to us. Please visit `www.packt.com/submit-errata`, selecting your book, clicking on the Errata Submission Form link, and entering the details.

Piracy: If you come across any illegal copies of our works in any form on the Internet, we would be grateful if you would provide us with the location address or website name. Please contact us at `copyright@packt.com` with a link to the material.

If you are interested in becoming an author: If there is a topic that you have expertise in and you are interested in either writing or contributing to a book, please visit `authors.packtpub.com`.

Reviews

Please leave a review. Once you have read and used this book, why not leave a review on the site that you purchased it from? Potential readers can then see and use your unbiased opinion to make purchase decisions, we at Packt can understand what you think about our products, and our authors can see your feedback on their book. Thank you!

For more information about Packt, please visit `packt.com`.

Introduction to ReasonML

The last decade has seen numerous paradigm shifts in the way we build user interfaces. Web applications have moved from server-side frameworks to client-side frameworks in order to provide better user experiences. Devices and browsers have become powerful enough to run robust client-side applications, and the JavaScript language itself has seen many improvements over the years. Progressive web apps provides a native-like user experience and WebAssembly allows for native-like performance on the web platform. An increasing number of applications are being built for the browser, resulting in larger client-side codebases needing to be maintained.

During this period, several frameworks, libraries, tools, and general best practices gained and then lost popularity, resulting in **JavaScript fatigue** for many developers. Companies are becoming increasingly cautious in committing to newer technologies due to their impact on hiring and retaining engineering talent, as well as productivity and maintainability. It can be an expensive mistake if you introduce the wrong technology (or the right technology at the wrong time) to your team.

For many companies and developers, React has proven to be a solid choice. In 2013, Facebook made the library open source after having used it internally since 2011. They challenged us to rethink best practices (https://www.youtube.com/watch?v=DgVS-zXgMTk feature=youtu.be) and it has since taken over frontend development (https://medium.freecodecamp.org/yes-react-is-taking-over-front-end-development-the-question-is-why-40837af8ab76). Encapsulating markup, behavior, and style into reusable components has become a huge productivity and maintainability win. The abstraction of the DOM has allowed for components to be simple, declarative functions of its props that are easy to reason about, compose, and test.

Via React, Facebook has done an incredible job educating the frontend-developer community on traditional functional programming paradigms that make it easier to reason about and maintain code. And now, Facebook believes the time is right for ReasonML.

This is a two-year chart from `npmtrends.com` that shows the number of weekly npm downloads for some of the top JavaScript libraries and frameworks. ReactJS looks to be a clear winner and has reached over 2,500,000 downloads per week:

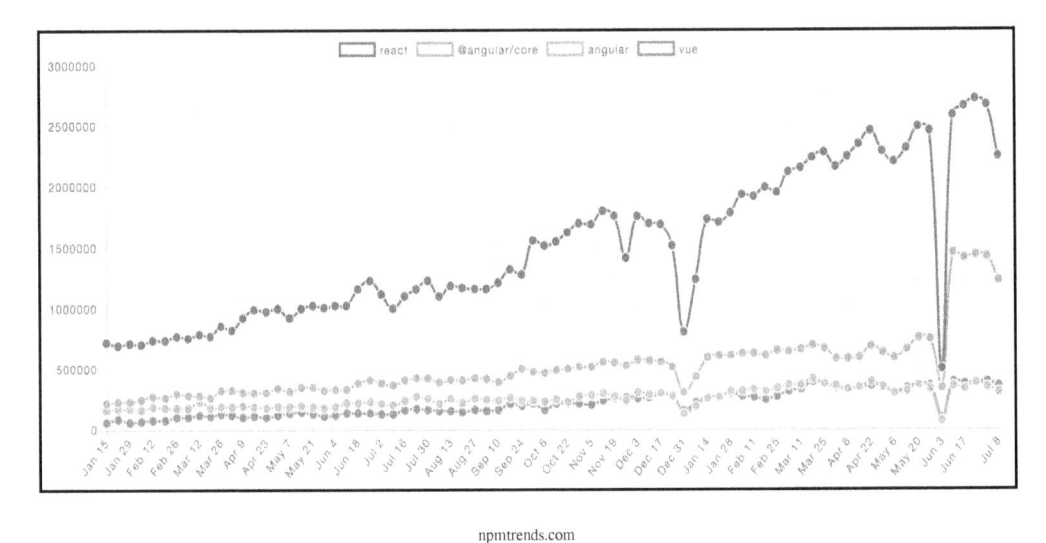

npmtrends.com

In this chapter, we'll do the following:

- Discuss what ReasonML is and what problems it tries to solve
- Understand some of the reasons why Facebook chose ReasonML as the future of ReactJS
- Experiment with ReasonML in an online playground and examine its compiled (JavaScript) output

What is ReasonML?

Reason is a layer of syntax & tooling on top of OCaml, a language Facebook uses actively. Jordan [Walke] started the concept of Reason before React, in fact. We're taking it and using it as an actual frontend language (among other uses) because we think that after three and half years, the React experiment has succeeded and people are now ready for Reason...

– Cheng Lou, January, 2017
(https://www.reactiflux.com/transcripts/cheng-lou/)

Chapter 1

Let's expand on this quote. ReasonML is not a new language; it's a new syntax for the OCaml language that is meant to be familiar to JavaScript developers. Reason, as we'll call it from now on, has the exact same AST as OCaml, so Reason and OCaml only differ by syntax. The semantics are the same. By learning Reason, you're also learning OCaml. In fact, there's a command-line tool that converts between OCaml and Reason syntax, called `refmt`, which formats Reason/OCaml code similar to JavaScript's prettier—in fact, prettier was inspired by `refmt`.

OCaml is a general-purpose programming language with an emphasis on expressiveness and safety. It was initially released in 1996 and has an advanced type system that helps catch your mistakes without getting in the way. Like JavaScript, OCaml features garbage collection for automatic memory management and first-class functions that can be passed around as arguments to other functions.

Reason is also a toolchain that makes getting started easier for those coming from a JavaScript background. This toolchain allows us to take advantage of both the JavaScript and OCaml ecosystems. We will dive deeper here in `Chapter 2`, *Setting Up a Development Environment*. For now, we'll experiment directly in the online playground by visiting Reason's online playground at `https://reasonml.github.io/try`.

Try typing in this Hello World example into the online playground:

```
let message = "World";
Js.log("Hello " ++ message);
```

There are two things you'll notice:

- The OCaml syntax is automatically generated in the lower-left section of the editor (not shown)
- The Reason/OCaml code is compiled to JavaScript directly in the browser:

  ```
  // Generated by BUCKLESCRIPT VERSION 3.2.0, PLEASE EDIT WITH CARE
  'use strict';

  var message = "World";

  console.log("Hello World");

  exports.message = message;
  /* Not a pure module */
  ```

[7]

You may be wondering how the Reason/OCaml code is being compiled from within the browser. BuckleScript, Reason's partner project, compiles the OCaml AST to JavaScript. Since Reason and OCaml both get converted into the same OCaml AST, BuckleScript supports both Reason and OCaml. Furthermore, since BuckleScript is itself written in OCaml, it can be compiled to JavaScript and run directly in the browser.

Inspecting the compiled JavaScript reveals just how readable it is. Looking closer, you'll notice that the compiled output has also been optimized: within the `console.log` statement, the `"Hello World"` string has been inlined directly instead of using the `message` variable.

> BuckleScript, using features of the OCaml type-system and compiler implementation is able to provide many optimizations during offline compilation, allowing the runtime code to be extremely fast.
>
> – *BuckleScript docs* (https://bucklescript.github.io/bucklescript/Manual.html#_why_bucklescript)

Notably, BuckleScript also supports string interpolation (https://bucklescript.github.io/docs/en/common-data-types.html#interpolation):

```
/* The message variable is interpolated */
{j|Hello $message|j}
```

Why Reason?

What makes Reason so compelling? What can Reason do that TypeScript or Flow cannot? Is it just about having a static type-checker? These are some of the questions I had when first getting started with Reason.

Support for immutability and purity

Reason isn't just about having a static type system. Also important is the fact that Reason is immutable by default. Immutability is an important concept in functional programming. In practice, using immutable data structures (data structures that can't change) results in safer, easier-to-reason-about, and more maintainable code than their mutable counterparts. This will be a recurring theme throughout this book.

Purity is another important concept in functional programming. A function is said to be pure if its output is determined only by its input, without observable side-effects. In other words, a pure function doesn't do anything outside of returning a value. The following is an example of a pure function:

```
let add = (a, b) => a + b;
```

And, this is an example of an impure function:

```
let add = (a, b) => {
  Js.log("side-effect");
  a + b;
};
```

The side-effect in this case is writing to the browser's console. That's why, in our preceding `Hello World` example, BuckleScript included the `/* Not a pure module */` comment at the end of the compiled output.

Mutating a global variable is also a side-effect. Consider the following JavaScript:

```
var globalObject = {total: 0};
const addAndMutate = (a, b) => globalObject.total = a + b;
addAndMutate(40, 2);
/* globalObject now is mutated */
```

The global object was mutated, and now its `total` property is `42`. We now have to be aware of all areas where this `globalObject` is mutated whenever using it. Forgetting that this object is both global and mutable can lead to hard-to-debug problems. One idiomatic solution to this problem is to move `globalObject` into a module where it's no longer global. This way, only that module has access to it. However, we'd still need to be aware of all areas within this module that can update the object.

If `globalObject` was immutable instead, there would be no way to mutate it. Therefore, we wouldn't need an awareness of all the areas that can mutate `globalObject`, since there wouldn't be any of these areas. We'll see that, with Reason, it's fairly simple and natural to build real applications in this way by creating updated copies of the original data. Consider the following:

```
let foo = 42;
let foo = foo + 1;
Js.log(foo);
/* 43 */
```

Introduction to ReasonML

The syntax feels quite natural. As we'll see later in this book, immutability—changing by returning updated copies instead of applying destructive changes in place—fits the React/Redux way of doing things quite well.

The original `foo` was not mutated; it was shadowed. Once shadowed, the old `foo` binding is unavailable. Bindings can be shadowed in local scopes as well as global scopes:

```
let foo = 42;

{
  let foo = 43;
  Js.log(foo); /* 43 */
};

Js.log(foo); /* 42 */

let foo = 43;
Js.log(foo); /* 43 */
```

Trying to mutate `foo` results in a compilation error:

```
let foo = 42;
foo = 43;
/* compilation error */
```

We can see that immutability and purity are related topics. Having a language that supports immutability allows you to program in a pure way without side-effects. However, what if there are times when purity would cause the code to become more complex and harder to reason about than using side-effects? You may be relieved to learn that Reason (interchangeable with OCaml throughout the rest of this book) is a pragmatic language that let's us cause side-effects when needed.

> *The key thing when using a language like [Reason] is not to avoid side-effects, because avoiding side-effects is equivalent to avoiding doing anything useful. It turns out, in reality, programs don't just compute things, they do things. They send messages and they write files and they do all sorts of stuff. The doing of things is automatically involving side-effects. The thing that a language which supports purity gives you, is it gives you the ability to, by and large, segment out the part that is side-effecting to clear and controlled areas of your code, and that makes it much easier to reason about.*
>
> *– Yaron Minsky*
> (https://www.youtube.com/watch?v=-J8YyfrSwTk&feature=youtu.be&t=47m29s)

It's also important to know that immutability doesn't come at the cost of performance. Under the hood, there are optimizations in place that keeps Reason's immutable data structures fast.

Module system

Reason has a sophisticated module system that allows for modular development and code organization. All modules are globally available in Reason, and module interfaces can be used to hide implementation details when needed. We will be exploring this concept in `Chapter 5`, *Effective ML*.

Type system

Reason's type system is sound, which means that, once compiled, there won't be runtime type errors. There is no `null` in the language, nor are there any bugs related to `null`. In JavaScript, when something is of the `number` type, it can also be `null`. Reason uses a special type for things that can also be `null`, and forces the developer to handle those cases appropriately by refusing to compile otherwise.

So far, we've already written some, albeit basic, Reason code without even talking about types. Reason infers types automatically. As we'll learn throughout this book, the type system is a tool that provides guarantees without getting in our way, and when used properly, can allow us to offload things to the compiler that we used to keep in our heads.

Reason's support for immutable programming, sound type system, and sophisticated module system are big parts of why Reason is so great, and there's something to be said about using all of these features together in one language that was built with these features in mind. When Facebook initially released React, they asked us to give it five minutes (`https://signalvnoise.com/posts/3124-give-it-five-minutes`) and, hopefully, that same frame of mind will pay off here as well.

Cross-platform

Building React applications with Reason is a lovely experience and, what's more, since OCaml is able to compile to native, we will be able to use these same skills to build apps that compile to assembly, iOS/Android, and much more. In fact, Jared Forsyth has already created a game called Gravitron (`https://github.com/jaredly/gravitron`) that compiles to iOS, Android, web, and macOS from one Reason codebase. That being said, the frontend JavaScript story is much more polished as of this writing.

Maintainability

Reason may take some time to get comfortable with, but you can think of this time as an investment in the maintenance and confidence of your future product. Although languages with gradual type systems, such as TypeScript, may be easier to get started with, they don't provide the sorts of guarantees that a sound type system such as Reason's can provide. Reason's true benefits cannot be completely conveyed within simple examples, and only really shine when they save you time and energy in reasoning about, refactoring, and maintaining your code. Put it this way; if someone told me they were 99% sure a spider wasn't in my bed, I would still have to check the entire bed because I don't like bugs!

As long as you're 100% in Reason and your code compiles, the type system guarantees there will be no runtime type errors. It's true that when you are interoperating with non-Reason code (JavaScript, for example), you introduce the possibility of runtime type errors. Reason's sound type system allows you to trust that the Reason parts of the application won't cause runtime type errors, which therefore allows you to focus extra attention on ensuring that these areas of the application are safe. In my experience, programming in a dynamic language can feel noticeably dangerous. Reason on the other hand feels like it always has your back.

Interoperability

That being said, sometimes—and especially when first learning about type systems—you may be unsure as to how to get your code to compile. Reason, through BuckleScript, allows you to drop down to raw JavaScript when you need to, either via bindings or directly inside your Reason (`.re`) files. This gives you the freedom to figure things out as you go along in JavaScript, and then once you're ready, convert that section of the code to type-safe Reason.

BuckleScript also lets us bind to idiomatic JavaScript in a very reasonable way. As you'll learn in `Chapter 4`, *BuckleScript, Belt, and Interoperability*, BuckleScript is an incredibly powerful part of Reason.

ES2030

Writing in Reason feels like writing in a future version of JavaScript. Some Reason language features, including the pipe operator (`https://github.com/tc39/proposal-pipeline-operator`) and pattern matching (`https://github.com/tc39/proposal-pattern-matching`), are currently being proposed to the TC39 Committee to add into the JavaScript language. With Reason, we can take advantage of these features, and much more, today.

Community

The Reason community is, hands down, one of the most helpful, supportive, and inclusive communities I've ever been a part of. If you have a question, or are stuck on something, the Reason Discord channel is the place to go for realtime support.

> Reason Discord channel:
>
> `https://discord.gg/reasonml`

Often, when starting with a new technology, talking to someone with experience for five minutes can save you hours of frustration. I've personally asked questions at all hours of the day (and night) and am so incredibly grateful for and amazed by how quickly someone helps me out. Take a moment to join the Discord channel, introduce yourself, ask questions, and share your feedback on how to make Reason better!

The Future of ReactJS

In practice, few real-world applications use just ReactJS. Additional technologies, such as Babel, ESLint, Redux, Flow/TypeScript, and Immutable.js, are typically brought in to help increase the maintainability of a codebase. Reason replaces the need for these additional technologies with its core language features.

ReasonReact is a Reason library that binds to ReactJS and provides a simpler, safer way to build ReactJS components. Just like ReactJS is just JavaScript, ReasonReact is just Reason. Additionally, it's easy to incrementally adopt because it was made by the same person who created ReactJS.

ReasonReact comes with a built in router, Redux-like data management, and JSX. You'll feel quite at home coming from a ReactJS background.

It's important to mention that Reason/ReasonReact is already being used by several companies in production, including within one of the largest codebases in the world. Facebook's messenger.com codebase is already over 50% converted to ReasonReact.

> *Every ReasonReact feature has been extensively tested on the messenger.com codebase.*
>
> *– Cheng Lou*
> (`https://reason.town/reason-philosophy`)

As a result, new releases of Reason and ReasonReact come with code mods that automate much, if not all, of the upgrade process for your code base. New features are thoroughly tested internally at Facebook before they're released to the public, and this results in a pleasant developer experience.

Exploring Reason

Ask yourself whether the following is a statement or an expression:

```
let foo = "bar";
```

In JavaScript, it's a statement, but in Reason, it's an expression. Another example of an expression is `4 + 3`, which can also be represented as `4 + (2 + 1)`.

Many things in Reason are expressions, including control structures such as `if-else`, `switch`, `for` and `while`:

```
let message = if (true) {
  "Hello"
} else {
  "Goodbye"
};
```

We also have ternaries in Reason. Here is another way to express the preceding code:

```
let message = true ? "Hello" : "Goodbye";
```

Even anonymous block scopes are expressions that evaluate to the last line's expression:

```
let message = {
  let part1 = "Hello";
  let part2 = "World";
  {j|$part1 $part2|j};
};
/* message evaluates to "Hello World" */
/* part1 and part2 are not accessible here */
```

A `tuple` is an immutable data structure that can hold different types of values and can be of any length:

```
let tuple = ("one", 2, "three");
```

Let's use what we know so far and dive right in with the `FizzBuzz` example from Reason's online playground. `FizzBuzz` was a popular interview question to determine whether a candidate is able to code. The challenge is to write a problem that prints the numbers from `1` to `100`, but instead prints `Fizz` for multiples of three, `Buzz` for multiples of five, and `FizzBuzz` for multiples of both three and five:

```
/* Based on https://rosettacode.org/wiki/FizzBuzz#OCaml */
let fizzbuzz = (i) =>
  switch (i mod 3, i mod 5) {
  | (0, 0) => "FizzBuzz"
  | (0, _) => "Fizz"
  | (_, 0) => "Buzz"
  | _ => string_of_int(i)
  };

for (i in 1 to 100) {
  Js.log(fizzbuzz(i))
};
```

Here, `fizzbuzz` is a function that accepts an integer and returns a string. An imperative `for` loop logs its output to the console.

In Reason, a function's last expression becomes the function's return value. The `switch` expression is the only `fizzbuzz` expression, so whatever that evaluates to becomes the output of `fizzbuzz`. Like JavaScript, the `switch` evaluates an expression and the first matched case gets its branch executed. In this case, the `switch` evaluates the tuple expression: `(i mod 3, i mod 5)`.

Given `i=1`, `(i mod 3, i mod 5)` becomes `(1, 1)`. Since `(1, 1)` isn't matched by `(0, 0)`, `(0, _)`, or `(_, 0)`, in that order, the last case of `_` (that is, *anything*) is matched, and `"1"` is returned. Similarly, `fizzbuzz` returns `"2"` when given `i=2`. When given `i=3`, `"Fizz"` is returned.

Alternatively, we could have implemented `fizzbuzz` using `if-else`:

```
let fizzbuzz = (i) =>
  if (i mod 3 == 0 && i mod 5 == 0) {
    "FizzBuzz"
  } else if (i mod 3 == 0) {
    "Fizz"
  } else if (i mod 5 == 0) {
    "Buzz"
  } else {
    string_of_int(i)
  };
```

However, the switch version is much more readable. And as we'll see later in this chapter, the switch expression, also called **pattern matching**, is much more powerful than we've seen so far.

Data structures and types

A type is a set of values. More concretely, `42` has the `int` type because it's a value that's contained in the set of integers. A float is a number that includes a decimal point, that is, `42.` and `42.0`. In Reason, integers and floating point numbers have separate operators:

```
/* + for ints */
40 + 2;

/* +. for floats */
40. +. 2.;
```

The same is true for `-.`, `-`, `*.`, `*`, `/.`, and `/`.

Reason uses double quotes for the `string` type and single quotes for the `char` type.

Creating our own types

We can also create our types:

```
type person = (string, int);

/* or */

type name = string;
type age = int;
type person = (name, age);
```

Here's how we create a person of the `person` type:

```
let person = ("Zoe", 3);
```

We can also annotate any expression with its type:

```
let name = ("Zoe" : string);
let person = ((name, 3) : person);
```

Pattern matching

We can use pattern matching on our person:

```
switch (person) {
| ("Zoe", age) => {j|Zoe, $age years old|j}
| _ => "another person"
};
```

Let's use a record instead of a tuple for our person. Records are similar JavaScript objects except they're much lighter and are immutable by default:

```
type person = {
  age: int,
  name: string
};

let person = {
  name: "Zoe",
  age: 3
};
```

We can use pattern matching on records too:

```
switch (person) {
| {name: "Zoe", age} => {j|Zoe, $age years old|j}
| _ => "another person"
};
```

Like JavaScript, `{name: "Zoe", age: age}` can be represented as `{name: "Zoe", age}`.

We can create a new record from an existing one using the spread (...) operator:

```
let person = {...person, age: person.age + 1};
```

Records require type definitions before they can be used. Otherwise, the compiler will error with something like the following:

```
The record field name can't be found.
```

A record must be the same shape as its type. Therefore, we cannot add arbitrary fields to our `person` record:

```
let person = {...person, favoriteFood: "broccoli"};

/*
  We've found a bug for you!

  This record expression is expected to have type person
  The field favoriteFood does not belong to type person
*/
```

Tuples and records are examples of product types. In our recent examples, our `person` type required both an `int` and an `age`. Almost all of JavaScript's data structures are product types; one exception is the `boolean` type, which is either `true` or `false`.

Reason's variant type, which is an example of a sum type, allows us to express this or that. We can define the `boolean` type as a variant:

```
type bool =
  | True
  | False;
```

We can have as many constructors as we need:

```
type decision =
  | Yes
  | No
  | Maybe;
```

`Yes`, `No`, and `Maybe` are called constructors because we can use them to construct values. They're also commonly called **tags**. Because these tags can construct values, variants are both a type and a data structure:

```
let decision = Yes;
```

And, of course, we can pattern match on `decision`:

```
switch (decision) {
| Yes => "Let's go."
| No => "I'm staying here."
| Maybe => "Convince me."
};
```

Chapter 1

If we were to forget to handle a case, the compiler would warn us:

```
switch (decision) {
| Yes => "Let's go."
| No => "I'm staying here."
};

/*
  Warning number 8

  You forgot to handle a possible value here, for example:
  Maybe
*/
```

As we'll learn in `Chapter 2`, *Setting Up a Development Environment,* the compiler can be configured to turn this warning into an error. Let's see one way to help make our code more resilient to future refactors by taking advantage of these exhaustiveness checks.

Take the following example where we are tasked with calculating the price of a concert venue's seat given its section. Floor seats are $55, while all other seats are $45:

```
type seat =
  | Floor
  | Mezzanine
  | Balcony;

let getSeatPrice = (seat) =>
  switch(seat) {
  | Floor => 55
  | _ => 45
  };
```

If, later, the concert venue allows the sale of seats in the orchestra pit area for $65, we would first add another constructor to `seat`:

```
type seat =
  | Pit
  | Floor
  | Mezzanine
  | Balcony;
```

[19]

Introduction to ReasonML

However, due to the usage of the catch-all _ case, our compiler doesn't complain after this change. It would be much better if it did since that would help us during our refactoring process. Stepping through compiler messages after changing type definitions is how Reason (and the ML family of languages in general) makes refactoring and extending code a safer, more pleasant process. This is, of course, not limited to variant types. Adding another field to our `person` type would also result in the same process of stepping through compiler messages.

Instead, we should reserve using _ for an infinite number of cases (such as our `fizzbuzz` example). We can refactor `getSeatPrice` to use explicit cases instead:

```
let getSeatPrice = (seat) =>
  switch(seat) {
  | Floor => 55
  | Mezzanine | Balcony => 45
  };
```

Here, we welcome the compiler nicely informing us of our unhandled case and then add it:

```
let getSeatPrice = (seat) =>
  switch(seat) {
  | Pit => 65
  | Floor => 55
  | Mezzanine | Balcony => 45
  };
```

Let's now imagine that each seat, even ones in the same section (that is, ones that have the same tag) can have different prices. Well, Reason variants can also hold data:

```
type seat =
  | Pit(int)
  | Floor(int)
  | Mezzanine(int)
  | Balcony(int);

let seat = Floor(57);
```

And we can access this data with pattern matching:

```
let getSeatPrice = (seat) =>
  switch (seat) {
  | Pit(price)
  | Floor(price)
  | Mezzanine(price)
  | Balcony(price) => price
  };
```

Variants are not just limited to one piece of data. Let's imagine that we want our `seat` type to store its price as well as whether it's still available. If it's not available, it should store the ticket holder's information:

```
type person = {
  age: int,
  name: string,
};

type seat =
  | Pit(int, option(person))
  | Floor(int, option(person))
  | Mezzanine(int, option(person))
  | Balcony(int, option(person));
```

Before explaining what the `option` type is, let's have a look at its implementation:

```
type option('a)
  | None
  | Some('a);
```

The `'a` in the preceding code is called a **type variable**. Type variables always start with a `'`. This type definition uses a type variable so that it could work for any type. If it didn't, we would need to create a `personOption` type that would only work for the `person` type:

```
type personOption(person)
  | None
  | Some(person);
```

What if we wanted an option for another type as well? Instead of repeating this type declaration over and over, we declare a polymorphic type. A polymorphic type is a type that includes a type variable. The `'a` (pronounced alpha) type variable will be swapped with `person` in our example. Since this type definition is so common, it's included in Reason's standard library, so there's no need to declare the `option` type in your code.

Jumping back to our `seat` example, we store its price as an `int` and its holder as an `option(person)`. If there's no holder, it's still available. We could have an `isAvailable` function that would take a `seat` and return a `bool`:

```
let isAvailable = (seat) =>
  switch (seat) {
  | Pit(_, None)
  | Floor(_, None)
  | Mezzanine(_, None)
  | Balcony(_, None) => true
```

Introduction to ReasonML

```
  | _ => false
};
```

Let's take a step back and look at the implementations of getSeatPrice and isAvailable. It's a shame that both functions need to be aware of the different constructors when they don't have anything to do with the price or availability of the seat. Taking another look at our seat type, we see that (int, option(person)) is repeated for each constructor. Also, there isn't really a nice way to avoid using the _ case in isAvailable. These are all signs that another type definition might serve our needs better. Let's remove the arguments from the seat type and rename it section. We'll declare a new record type, called seat, with fields for section, price, and person:

```
type person = {
  age: int,
  name: string,
};

type section =
  | Pit
  | Floor
  | Mezzanine
  | Balcony;

type seat = {
  section, /* same as section: section, */
  price: int,
  person: option(person)
};

let getSeatPrice = seat -> seat.price;

let isAvailable = seat =>
  switch (seat.person) {
  | None => true
  | Some(_person) => false
  };
```

Now, our getSeatPrice and isAvailable functions have a higher signal-to-noise ratio, and don't need to change when the section type changes.

As a side note, _ is used to prefix a variable to prevent the compiler from warning us about the variable being unused.

Making Invalid States Impossible

Let's say that we'd like to add a field to `seat` to hold the date a seat was purchased:

```
type seat = {
  section,
  price: int,
  person: option(person),
  dateSold: option(string)
};
```

Now, we've introduced the possibility of an invalid state in our code. Here's an example of such a state:

```
let seat = {
  section: Pit,
  price: 42,
  person: None,
  dateSold: Some("2018-07-16")
};
```

In theory, the `dateSold` field should only hold a date when the `person` field holds a ticket holder. The ticket has a sold date, but no owner. We could look through our imaginary implementation to verify that this state would never happen, but there would still be the possibility that we missed something, or that some minor refactor introduced a bug that was overlooked.

Since we now have the power of Reason's type system at our disposal, let's offload this work to the compiler. We are going to use the type system to enforce invariants in our code. If our code breaks these rules, it won't compile.

One giveaway that this invalid state could exist is the use of `option` types within our record field. In these cases, there may be a way to use a variant instead such that each constructor only holds the relevant data. In our case, our sold-date and ticket-holder data should only exist when the seat has been sold:

```
type person = {
  age: int,
  name: string,
};

type date = string;

type section =
  | Pit
  | Floor
```

Introduction to ReasonML

```
  | Mezzanine
  | Balcony;

type status =
  | Available
  | Sold(date, person);

type seat = {
  section,
  price: int,
  status
};

let getSeatPrice = (seat) => seat.price;

let isAvailable = (seat) =>
  switch (seat.status) {
  | Available => true
  | Sold(_) => false
  };
```

Check out our new `status` type. The `Available` constructor holds no data, and `Sold` holds the sold date as well as the ticket holder.

With this `seat` type, there's no way to represent the previous invalid state of having a sold date without a ticket holder. It's also a good sign that our `seat` type no longer includes `option` types.

Summary

In this chapter, we got a feel for what Reason is and what problems it tries to solve. We saw how Reason's type inference removes much of the burden associated with statically-typed languages. We learned that the type system is a tool that can be used to provide codebases with powerful guarantees that provide an excellent developer experience. While Reason may take some time to get used to, it's well worth the investment for medium-sized to larger codebases.

In the next chapter, we'll learn about Reason's toolchain when we set up our development environment. In `Chapter 3`, *Creating ReasonReact Components*, we'll start to build an application that we'll use throughout the rest of this book. By the end of this book, you'll be comfortable building real-world React applications in Reason.

Setting Up a Development Environment

In addition to being a new syntax for OCaml, Reason is a toolchain that makes it easy to get started. In this chapter, we'll do the following:

- Learn about the Reason toolchain
- Configure our editor
- Use `bsb` to start a pure Reason project
- Learn about `bsconfig.json`
- Write an example pure Reason application that manipulates the DOM
- Use `bsb` to start a ReasonReact project
- Get comfortable using `webpack` within a Reason project

To follow along, clone this book's GitHub repository and start from this chapter's directory. You're also welcome to start from a blank project:

```
git clone https://github.com/PacktPublishing/ReasonML-Quick-Start-Guide.git
cd ReasonML-Quick-Start-Guide
cd Chapter02/pure-reason-start
npm install
```

This chapter is meant to get you comfortable with the Reason toolchain. We'll have separate development environments for the pure Reason project and the ReasonReact one. After following along, you'll be comfortable enough to tweak the development environment to your liking. Don't worry about messing anything up, since we'll start fresh in Chapter 3, *Creating ReasonReact Components*, from another directory.

Setting Up a Development Environment

The Reason toolchain

At the time of writing, the Reason toolchain is essentially BuckleScript—Reason's partner project—and the familiar JavaScript toolchain, namely `npm` and `webpack` (or another JavaScript module bundler).

There's no longer a need for `babel`, since BuckleScript compiles to the ES5 version of JavaScript. The compiled output can be configured to use either the CommonJS, AMD, or ES module formats. Reason's powerful static-type system replaces the need for Flow and ESlint. Additionally, Reason's editor plugins all come with `refmt`, which is essentially `prettier` for Reason.

Installing BuckleScript

BuckleScript is a compiler that takes the OCaml AST and emits clean, readable, and performant JavaScript. It can be installed via `npm`, as follows:

```
npm install -g bs-platform
```

Installing `bs-platform` provides a binary called `bsb`, which is BuckleScript's build system.

> In the future, the Reason toolchain will make it much easier to target native platforms as well as JavaScript. Currently, Reason compiles to native by using a fork of `bsb`, called `bsb-native`.

Editor configuration

Reason supports a variety of editors, including VSCode, Sublime Text, Atom, Vim, and Emacs. VSCode is the recommended editor. To configure VSCode, simply install the `reason-vscode` extension. That's it!

See the documentation for editor-specific instructions.

> The Reason editor support documentation can be found at https://reasonml.github.io/docs/editor-plugins.

Setting up a pure Reason project

The `bsb` binary includes a project generator. We'll use it to create a pure Reason project using the `basic-reason` theme. Run `bsb -themes` to see all available project templates:

```
Available themes:
basic
basic-reason
generator
minimal
node
react
react-lite
tea
```

Since BuckleScript works with both OCaml and Reason, some themes are only for OCaml projects. That being said, feel free to mix OCaml's `.ml` files with Reason's `.re` files within any BuckleScript project.

In this chapter, we'll focus on using the `basic-reason` and `react` templates. If you're curious, the `react-lite` theme is like the `react` one, except `webpack` is replaced with a simpler, faster, and more reliable module bundler that is intended only for development purposes.

Let's first create a pure Reason project:

```
bsb -init my-first-app -theme basic-reason
cd my-first-app
```

When we open the project in our editor, we see the following project structure:

```
├── .gitignore
├── README.md
├── bsconfig.json
├── node_modules
│   ├── .bin
│   │   ├── bsb
│   │   ├── bsc
│   │   └── bsrefmt
│   └── bs-platform
├── package.json
└── src
    └── Demo.re
```

Overall, there isn't much here, which is kind of refreshing coming from JavaScript. In `node_modules`, we see `bs-platform` along with some binaries:

- `bsb`: The build system
- `bsc`: The compiler
- `bsrefmt`: This is essentially JavaScript's `prettier`, but for Reason

As we'll soon see, the `bsb` binary is used within `npm` scripts. This `bsc` binary is rarely used directly. The `bsrefmt` binary is used by editor plugins.

In `Demo.re`, we see a simple log message:

```
/* Demo.re */
Js.log("Hello, BuckleScript and Reason!");
```

`package.json` looks somewhat familiar. The `scripts` field shows our currently available `npm` scripts:

```
/* package.json */
{
  "name": "my-first-app",
  "version": "0.1.0",
  "scripts": {
    "build": "bsb -make-world",
    "start": "bsb -make-world -w",
    "clean": "bsb -clean-world"
  },
  "keywords": [
    "BuckleScript"
  ],
  "author": "",
  "license": "MIT",
  "devDependencies": {
    "bs-platform": "^4.0.5"
  }
}
```

Run `npm run build` to compile `Demo.re` to JavaScript. By default, the compiled output appears right beside the source file as `Demo.bs.js`. How does it know which files to compile, and where to output them? That's where `bsconfig.json` comes in.

The bsconfig.json file

The `bsconfig.json` file is a required file for all BuckleScript projects. Let's explore it:

```
// This is the configuration file used by BuckleScript's build system bsb.
// Its documentation lives here:
http://bucklescript.github.io/bucklescript/docson/#build-schema.json
// BuckleScript comes with its own parser for bsconfig.json, which is
normal JSON, with the extra support of comments and trailing commas.
{
  "name": "my-first-app",
  "version": "0.1.0",
  "sources": {
    "dir" : "src",
    "subdirs" : true
  },
  "package-specs": {
    "module": "commonjs",
    "in-source": true
  },
  "suffix": ".bs.js",
  "bs-dependencies": [
      // add your dependencies here. You'd usually install them normally
through `npm install my-dependency`. If my-dependency has a bsconfig.json
too, then everything will work seamlessly.
  ],
  "warnings": {
    "error" : "+101"
  },
  "namespace": true,
  "refmt": 3
}
```

Setting Up a Development Environment

We'll soon be changing some of these defaults to get more comfortable with BuckleScript's configuration file. Let's first add the following code to `Demo.re`:

```
type decision =
  | Yes
  | No
  | Maybe;

let decision = Maybe;

let response =
  switch (decision) {
  | Yes => "Yes!"
  | No => "I'm afraid not."
  };

Js.log(response);
```

As you can see, the `switch` expression isn't handling all possible cases of `decision`. Running `npm run build` results in the following output:

```
ninja: Entering directory `lib/bs'
[3/3] Building src/Demo.mlast.d
[1/1] Building src/Demo-MyFirstApp.cmj

  Warning number 8
  .../Demo.re 9:3-12:3
   7 |
   8 | let response =
   9 | switch (decision) {
  10 | | Yes => "Yes!"
  11 | | No => "I'm afraid not."
  12 | };
  13 |
  14 | Js.log(response);
  You forgot to handle a possible value here, for example:
Maybe
```

[30]

The warnings field

If we wanted to force this warning to throw an error instead, we note the error number from the preceding snippet and change the `warnings` field of `bsconfig.json` to the following:

```
"warnings": {
  "error": "+101+8" // added "+8"
},
```

To turn all warnings into errors, use the following code:

```
"warnings": {
  "error": "A"
},
```

> For a complete list of warning numbers, check out https://caml.inria.fr/pub/docs/manual-ocaml/comp.html#sec281 (scroll down a bit).

The package-specs field

The `package-specs` field contains two fields: `module` and `in-source`.

The `module` field controls the JavaScript module format. The default is `commonjs`, and other available options include `amdjs`, `amdjs-global`, `es6`, and `es6-global`. The `-global` part tells BuckleScript to resolve `node_modules` to relative paths for browsers.

The `in-source` field controls the destination of the generated JavaScript files; `true` results in the generated files being placed along side source files, and `false` results in the generated files being placed in `lib/js`. Setting `in-source` to `false` is useful when using Reason within an existing JavaScript project so that the existing build pipeline can be used without having to change.

Let's use the `"es6"` module format for now, and place our compiled assets in `lib/js`:

```
"package-specs": {
  "module": "es6",
  "in-source": false
},
```

The suffix field

The `suffix` field configures the extension of the generated JavaScript files. It's generally best to keep the `".bs.js"` suffix since this helps `bsb` better track the generated artifacts.

The sources field

BuckleScript knew to look in the `src` directory because of the following configuration:

```
"sources": {
  "dir" : "src",
  "subdirs" : true
},
```

If `subdirs` were `false`, any `.re` and `.ml` files located in subdirectories of `src` wouldn't be compiled.

> For more information regarding `bsconfig.json`, see the following section of the BuckleScript documentation: https://bucklescript.github.io/docs/build-configuration.

Working with DOM

Let's try working with the DOM in pure Reason before jumping into ReasonReact. We'll write a module that does the following:

- Creates a DOM element
- Sets the `innerText` of that element
- Appends that element to the body of the document

Create an `index.html` file in the project's root with the following content:

```
<html>
  <head></head>
  <body>
    <!-- if "in-source": false -->
    <script type="module" src="lib/es6/src/Demo.bs.js"></script>

    <!-- if "in-source": true -->
    <!-- <script type="module" src="src/Demo.bs.js"></script> -->
  </body>
</html>
```

Notice the `type="module"` attribute on the `script` tag. If all module dependencies are **ES Module (ESM)** compliant, and they are all available from within the browser, you don't need a module bundler to get started (assuming you're using a browser that supports ES modules).

In `Greeting.re`, add the following greeting function:

```
let greeting = name => {j|hello $name|j};
```

And in `Demo.re`, add the following code:

```
[@bs.val] [@bs.scope "document"]
external createElement : string => Dom.element = "";

[@bs.set] external setInnerText : (Dom.element, string) => unit =
"innerText";

[@bs.val] [@bs.scope "document.body"]
external appendChild : Dom.element => Dom.element = "";

let div = createElement("div");
setInnerText(div, Greeting.greeting("world"));
appendChild(div);
```

Using BuckleScript's powerful interoperability features (which we will dive into in Chapter 4, *BuckleScript, Belt and Interoperability*) the preceding code binds to existing browser APIs, namely `document.createElement`, `innerText`, and `document.body.appendChild`, and then uses those bindings to create a `div` with some text that is appended to the body of the document.

Run `npm run build`, start a server (perhaps with `php -S localhost:3000` in a new console tab) at the root of the project, and then navigate to `http://localhost:3000` to see our newly-created DOM element:

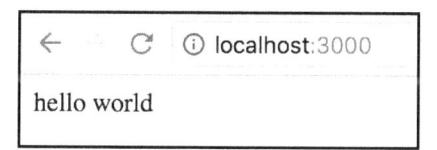

hello world

Setting Up a Development Environment

The takeaway is that having to work with the DOM in this way is really tedious. It's hard to type DOM APIs due to JavaScript's dynamic nature. For example, `Element.innerText` is used both to get and set an element's `innerText`, depending on how it's used, which therefore would result in two different type signatures:

```
[@bs.get] external getInnerText: Dom.element => string = "innerText";
[@bs.set] external setInnerText : (Dom.element, string) => unit = "innerText";
```

Luckily, we have React, which largely abstracts the DOM for us. Using React, we don't need to worry about typing the DOM APIs. It's nice to know that when we want to interact with various browser APIs, BuckleScript has the tools we need to get the job done. While it's certainly possible to write frontend web applications in pure Reason, it's a much more pleasant experience when using ReasonReact, especially when first getting started with Reason.

Setting up a ReasonReact project

To create a new ReasonReact project, run the following command:

```
bsb -init my-reason-react-app -theme react
cd my-reason-react-app
```

After opening our text editor, we see that a couple of things have changed. The `package.json` file lists the relevant React and webpack dependencies. Let's install them:

```
npm install
```

We also have the following webpack-related npm scripts:

```
"webpack": "webpack -w",
"webpack:production": "NODE_ENV=production webpack"
```

In `bsconfig.json`, we have a new field that turns on JSX for ReasonReact:

```
"reason": {
  "react-jsx": 2
},
```

We have a simple `webpack.config.js` file:

```
const path = require("path");
const outputDir = path.join(__dirname, "build/");

const isProd = process.env.NODE_ENV === "production";

module.exports = {
  entry: "./src/Index.bs.js",
  mode: isProd ? "production" : "development",
  output: {
    path: outputDir,
    publicPath: outputDir,
    filename: "Index.js"
  }
};
```

Note how the configured entry point is `"./src/Index.bs.js"`, which makes sense since, by default, `"in-source"` is set to `true` in `bsconfig.json`. The rest is just normal webpack stuff.

To run this project, we need to run both `bsb` and `webpack`:

```
npm start

/* in another shell */
npm run webpack

/* in another shell */
php -S localhost:3000
```

Since the `index.html` file is located within the `src` directory, we visit `http://localhost:3000/src` to see the default application.

Improving the developer experience

Now that we've seen how the toolchain works at a basic level, let's improve our developer experience so that we can start our project with just one command. We'll need to install a couple of dependencies, as follows:

```
npm install webpack-dev-server --save-dev
npm install npm-run-all --save-dev
```

Setting Up a Development Environment

Now, we can update our npm scripts:

```
"scripts": {
  "start": "npm-run-all --parallel start:*",
  "start:bsb": "bsb -clean-world -make-world -w",
  "start:webpack": "webpack-dev-server --port 3000",
  "build": "npm-run-all build:*",
  "build:bsb": "bsb -clean-world -make-world",
  "build:webpack": "NODE_ENV=production webpack",
  "test": "echo \"Error: no test specified\" && exit 1"
},
```

Next, to get `webpack-dev-server` to serve the `index.html` file on `http://localhost:3000` instead of `http://localhost:3000/src`, we need to install and configure `HtmlWebpackPlugin`:

npm install html-webpack-plugin --save-dev

We can remove the default `<script src="../build/Index.js"></script>` tag in `src/index.html`, since `HTMLWebpackPlugin` will insert the script tag automatically.

We also remove the `publicPath` setting so that the default path of `"/"` will be used:

```
const path = require("path");
const HtmlWebpackPlugin = require("html-webpack-plugin");

const isProd = process.env.NODE_ENV === "production";

module.exports = {
  entry: "./src/Index.bs.js",
  mode: isProd ? "production" : "development",
  output: {
    path: path.join(__dirname, "build/"),
    filename: "Index.js"
  },
  plugins: [
    new HtmlWebpackPlugin({
      template: "./src/index.html"
    })
  ]
};
```

Now, we run `npm start` and visit `http://localhost:3000` to see the same ReasonReact application running.

Summary

In this chapter, we saw just how easy it is to get started with Reason. In Chapter 3, *Creating ReasonReact Components*, we'll start to build a ReasonReact application that we'll use throughout this book. This application will help to provide context as we learn more about Reason semantics, BuckleScript interoperability, and ReasonReact specifics.

Don't worry if you don't yet understand everything within these generated projects. By the end of Chapter 3, *Creating ReasonReact Components*, you'll be a lot more comfortable. However, if you have questions along the way, please don't hesitate to reach out on Reason's Discord channel for real-time assistance: https://discord.gg/reasonml.

I hope you'll find the Reason community as welcoming and helpful as I have.

3
Creating ReasonReact Components

Now that we've set up our development environment, we're ready to get started with ReasonReact—the future of ReactJS. Both ReasonML and ReasonReact were built by the same person who built ReactJS. ReasonReact is just Reason, much like how ReactJS is just JavaScript. Throughout the rest of this book, we will be working with an application that we will start building in this chapter. The following are screenshots of what we'll have built by the end of this chapter:

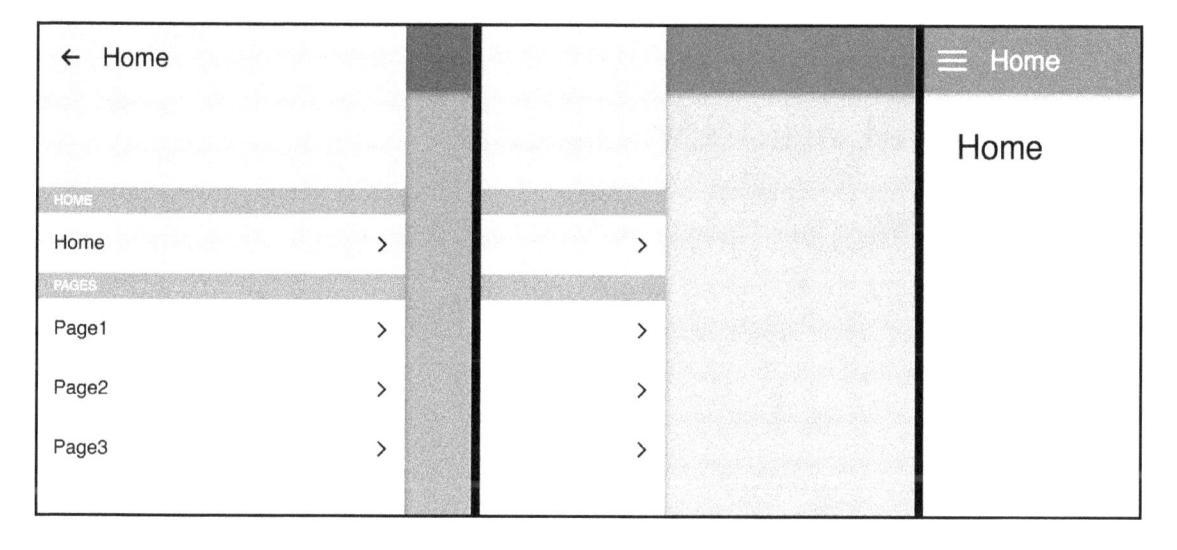

Creating ReasonReact Components

To follow along, clone this book's GitHub repository and start from Chapter03/start. Throughout the rest of this book, each directory shares the same development environment as the one we set up at the end of Chapter 2, *Setting Up a Development Environment*.

```
git clone https://github.com/PacktPublishing/ReasonML-Quick-Start-Guide.git
cd ReasonML-Quick-Start-Guide
cd Chapter03/start
npm install
```

We'll first explore ReasonReact, and at about halfway through this chapter, we'll shift to the Chapter03/app-start directory, where we'll start building an application with ReasonReact's built-in router.

In this chapter, we will do the following:

- Explore creating stateless and stateful ReasonReact components
- Create an application that includes navigation and routing
- See how so many of the ReactJS concepts you're already familiar with map nicely to ReasonReact
- Learn how ReasonReact can help us create more robust components thanks to Reason's type system

Component creation basics

Let's start by analyzing a simple stateless component. In App.re, let's render a `<div />` element with some text:

```
let component = ReasonReact.statelessComponent("App");

let make = _children => {
  ...component,
  render: _self => <div> {ReasonReact.string("hello world")} </div>,
};
```

And in Index.re, render the component to a DOM element with an ID of "root":

```
ReactDOMRe.renderToElementWithId(<App />, "root");
```

Due to Reason's module system, we do not need an `import` statement in Index.re nor an export statement in App.re. Every Reason file is a module, and every Reason module is globally available. Later in this book, we will see how a module's implementation details can be hidden so that users of your component only access things they are supposed to access.

Component templates

In ReasonReact, all components are created with one of the following four functions:

- `ReasonReact.statelessComponent`
- `ReasonReact.statelessComponentWithRetainedProps`
- `ReasonReact.reducerComponent`
- `ReasonReact.reducerComponentWithRetainedProps`

Each of the four functions accepts a `string` and returns a `record` corresponding to a different component template. The `string` argument is only for debugging purposes. The component gets its name (`<App />`) from its filename (`App.re`). The fields the returned record contains are dependent on which of the functions was used. In the case of our previous example, we have the following fields that we can override:

- `render`
- `didMount`
- `willReceiveProps`
- `shouldUpdate`
- `willUpdate`
- `didUpdate`
- `willUnmount`

Aside from the `render` field, the rest are just familiar ReactJS life cycle events. To override a field, add that field within the `make` function's returned `record`. In the preceding example, the component template's `render` field was replaced with the custom `render` function.

The `make` function accepts `props` as arguments, and returns a `record` of the same shape as the one that was initially created by one of the four component creation functions. The last argument to the `make` function must be the `children` prop. You may have noticed that `children` is prefixed with an _ in the preceding example. If your component does not need a reference to the children prop, then prefixing the argument with an _ prevents a compiler warning for the unused binding.

It may not appear immediately obvious, but the `make` function's curly braces belong to the returned `record` literal. The ...`component` expression spreads the contents of the original `record` in this new `record` so that individual fields can be overridden without having to explicitly set each field.

self

The `render` field holds a callback function that accepts an argument called `self`, and returns a value of type `ReasonReact.reactElement`. The three fields of the `self` record are the following:

- `state`
- `handle`
- `send`

By choice, ReasonReact does not have the concept of JavaScript's `this`. Instead, `self` holds the necessary information and is provided to callbacks that need it. We'll see more of `self` when using stateful components.

Event handlers

In our render function, we can attach event listeners to DOM elements the same way that we would in ReactJS. For example, to listen for the click event, we add an `onClick` attribute and set its value to an event handler:

```
let component = ReasonReact.statelessComponent("App");

let make = _children => {
  ...component,
  render: _self =>
    <div onClick={_event => Js.log("clicked")}>
      {ReasonReact.string("hello world")}
    </div>,
};
```

However, this callback function must accept exactly one argument (corresponding to a JavaScript DOM event) and must return a type called `unit`.

unit

In Reason, `unit` is a type that means "nothing." A function whose return type is `unit` cannot return anything other than `unit`. There is exactly one value of type `unit`: `()` (that is, a pair of empty parentheses, which is also called `unit`).

In contrast, there are exactly two values of type `bool`: `true` and `false`. There are an infinite number of values of type `int`.

As discussed in Chapter 1, *Introduction to ReasonML*, the idiomatic way to represent a nullable value in Reason is with the `option` type. The major difference between the `option` type and the `unit` type is that a value of type `option` could be nothing, or it could be some value where as a value of type `unit` is always `()`.

A function that accepts and/or returns `unit` likely causes side effects. For example, `Js.log` is a function that returns `unit`. The `onClick` event handler is also a function that returns `unit`.

`Random.bool` is an example of a function that accepts `unit` as its argument and returns a `bool`. The syntax for calling a function with `unit` is quite familiar:

```
Random.bool()
```

Since `onClick` needs a function that returns `unit`, the following will result in a type error:

```
let component = ReasonReact.statelessComponent("App");

let make = _children => {
  ...component,
  render: _self =>
    <div onClick={_event => 42}> {ReasonReact.string("hello world")}
  </div>,
};
```

The type error is shown here:

```
Error: This expression has type int but an expression was expected of type
    unit
```

In the error message, `This expression` refers to `42`.

JSX

Reason comes with the JSX syntax. One difference in ReasonReact's version of JSX is that we cannot do the following in ReasonReact:

```
<div>"hello world"</div>
```

Instead, we need to convert the `string` to a `ReasonReact.reactElement` with the `ReasonReact.string` function:

```
<div>ReasonReact.string("hello world")</div>
```

Creating ReasonReact Components

However, this still doesn't work. We need to also wrap the expression with { } to help the parser differentiate between multiple possible children:

```
<div> {ReasonReact.string("hello world")} </div>
```

You're free to create an alias that is less verbose and use that instead:

```
let str = ReasonReact.string;
<div> {str("hello world")} </div>;
```

When a custom component is invoked in JSX, its `make` function is called. The `<App />` syntax desugars to the following:

```
ReasonReact.element(App.make([|||]))
```

When a component will receive new props, its `make` function will again be called with the new props as arguments. The `make` function is like a combination of ReactJS's `constructor` and ReactJS's `componentWillReceiveProps`.

Props

Let's add a few props to our `<App />` component:

```
let make = (~greeting, ~name, _children) => {
  ...component,
  render: _self => <div> {ReasonReact.string(greeting ++ " " ++ name)}
</div>,
};
```

After compiling, we get a compiler error, because in `Index.re` we aren't providing the required `greeting` and `name` props:

```
We've found a bug for you!
1 | ReactDOMRe.renderToElementWithId(<App />, "root");
This call is missing arguments of type:
(~greeting: string),
(~name: string)
```

`greeting` and `name` are **labelled arguments** of the `make` function, meaning that they can be provided in any order. To convert an argument to a labelled argument, prefix it with a tilde (~). Reason also supports optional arguments as well as arguments with defaults. Let's give `greeting` a default value and make `name` optional:

```
let make = (~greeting="hello", ~name=?, _children) => {
  ...component,
```

```
  render: _self => {
    let name =
      switch (name) {
      | None => ""
      | Some(name) => name
      };
    <div> {ReasonReact.string(greeting ++ " " ++ name)} </div>;
  },
};
```

Since `name` is an optional argument, it's wrapped in an `option` type, and we can then pattern match on its value. Of course, this is just a long-winded way of providing `name` with a default argument of `""`.

Now, our example compiles even if `<App />` isn't provided with any props:

```
ReactDOMRe.renderToElementWithId(<App />, "root");
/* hello */

ReactDOMRe.renderToElementWithId(
  <App greeting="welcome," name="reason" />,
  "root",
);
/* welcome, reason */
```

If we then decide to remove the name prop, the compiler will tell us where we need to update the usage of `<App />`. This gives us the freedom to refactor our components without worrying about forgetting to update an area of our codebase. The compiler has our back!

Children

The last argument to the `make` function is always the `children` prop—it's mandatory. Just like other props, children can be any data structure. As long as the component allows it, we can use the render prop pattern that is popular in ReactJS. Importantly, ReasonReact always wraps children in an array, so we need to unwrap the array with the ... syntax if we don't want this wrapping.

In `App.re`, we'll remove all props except for the required `children` prop. In the render function, we invoke children with our hardcoded greeting:

```
/* App.re */
let component = ReasonReact.statelessComponent("App");
```

Creating ReasonReact Components

```
let make = children => {
  ...component,
  render: _self => children("hello"),
};
```

And in `Index.re`, we add a function as a child of `<App />` that accepts the provided greeting and returns JSX (which is of type `ReasonReact.reactElement`). Notice the `...` syntax used to unwrap the array that all ReasonReact children are wrapped with:

```
/* Index.re */
ReactDOMRe.renderToElementWithId(
  <App> ...{greeting => <div> {ReasonReact.string(greeting)} </div>}
  </App>,
  "root",
);
```

If we forget the `...`, the compiler will kindly let us know:

```
We've found a bug for you!

1 | ReactDOMRe.renderToElementWithId(
2 | <App> {greeting => <div> {ReasonReact.string(greeting)} </div>} </App>,
3 | "root",
4 | );

This has type:
  array('a)
But somewhere wanted:
  string => ReasonReact.reactElement
```

We'll even get a similar compiler message if we don't include any children (that is, just `<App />`), since that translates into an empty array. This means that we're guaranteed that users of our component have to provide a function of type `string => ReasonReact.reactElement` as a child of `<App />` if it's going to type check.

We can also mandate that our component accepts other children types, for example, a tuple of two strings:

```
/* App.re */
let component = ReasonReact.statelessComponent("App");

let make = children => {
  ...component,
  render: _self => {
    let (greeting, name) = children;
    <div> {ReasonReact.string(greeting ++ " " ++ name)} </div>;
  },
```

```
};

/* Index.re */
ReactDOMRe.renderToElementWithId(<App> ...("hello", "tuple") </App>,
"root");
```

Reason is able to infer that children must be a tuple of type (`string, string`) because of its use in `App.re`. For example, consider the following usage:

```
ReactDOMRe.renderToElementWithId(<App> ("hello") </App>, "root");
```

This will result in a friendly compiler error because the `App` component requires its children to be a tuple but the `App` component's children is not a tuple.

```
We've found a bug for you!
1 | ReactDOMRe.renderToElementWithId(<App> ("hello") </App>, "root");

This has type:
  array('a)
But somewhere wanted:
  (string, string)
```

This is incredibly powerful. Since we get these guarantees at compile time, we don't have to worry about runtime checks on the shape of our component's children. Similarly, we are guaranteed that props type check at compile time. Refactoring components is much less stressful because the compiler guides us along the way. What's more, thanks to Reason's powerful type inference, we haven't had to explicitly annotate any types so far.

Life cycles

ReasonReact supports the familiar ReactJS life cycle events. We will get a closer look at some of the life cycle events as we build our app, but, for now, let's see how we can implement ReactJS's `componentDidMount` life cycle hook for `<App />`:

```
let make = _children => {
  ...component,
  didMount: _self => Js.log("mounted"),
  render: _self => <div> {ReasonReact.string("hello")} </div>,
};
```

Creating ReasonReact Components

Instead of `componentDidMount`, we use `didMount`. Again, `didMount` is just a field within a record returned by the component's `make` function. The type of `didMount` is `self => unit`, which is a function that accepts `self` and returns `unit`. Since it returns `unit`, it's likely that `didMount` causes a side effect, and in our example it does. Running this in the browser results in `mounted` logged to the console.

Subscriptions helper

To make writing cleanup code more convenient and easier to remember, ReasonReact provides `self.onUnmount`, which can be used directly within a component's `didMount` life cycle (or anywhere that has access to `self`). This allows you to write the cleanup code alongside its complement instead of separately, within `willUnmount`:

```
didMount: self => {
  let intervalId = Js.Global.setInterval(() => Js.log("hello!"), 1000);
  self.onUnmount(() => Js.Global.clearInterval(intervalId));
},
```

Stateful components

So far, we've only used the `ReasonReact.statelessComponent` template. To create a stateful component, we switch out the component template to `ReasonReact.reducerComponent` and override some additional fields within the record returned by its `make` function. As we'll soon see, we'll also need to declare custom type definitions for use in these additional fields. It's called `reducerComponent` because it has the concept of state, actions, and reducers built in—just like Redux, except state, actions, and reducers are local to the component.

A simple counter component with buttons to increment and decrement the current count is shown here:

```
type state = int;

type action =
  | Increment
  | Decrement;

let component = ReasonReact.reducerComponent("App");

let make = _children => {
  ...component,
```

```
    initialState: () => 0,
    reducer: (action, state) =>
      switch (action) {
      | Increment => ReasonReact.Update(state + 1)
      | Decrement => ReasonReact.Update(state - 1)
      },
    render: self =>
      <>
        <button onClick={_event => self.send(Decrement)}>
          {ReasonReact.string("-")}
        </button>
        <span> {ReasonReact.string(string_of_int(self.state))} </span>
        <button onClick={_event => self.send(Increment)}>
          {ReasonReact.string("+")}
        </button>
      </>,
  };
```

The ReactJS Fragment syntax (`<>` and `</>`) is used here to wrap the `<button>` and `<span>` elements without adding an unnecessary DOM node.

State, action, and reducer

Let's break this down. At the top of the file, we see two type declarations, one for state and one for actions. The names `state` and `action` are a convention, but you can use any name you like:

```
type state = int;

type action =
  | Increment
  | Decrement;
```

Just as in Redux, events trigger actions that are sent to a reducer that then updates state. Next, the button's click event triggers a `Decrement` action that gets sent to the component's reducer via `self.send`. Remember, the render function is provided `self` as its argument:

```
<button onClick={_event => self.send(Increment)}>
  {ReasonReact.string("+")}
</button>
```

Creating ReasonReact Components

The `state` type declaration defines the shape of our state. In this case, our state is just an integer that holds the component's current count. The component's initial state is 0:

```
initialState: () => 0,
```

`initialState` requires a function of type `unit => state`.

When triggered by an action, the reducer function accepts that action as well as the current state, and returns a new state. Pattern matching is used on the current action, and `ReasonReact.Update` is used to return a new state:

```
reducer: (action, state) =>
  switch (action) {
  | Increment => ReasonReact.Update(state + 1)
  | Decrement => ReasonReact.Update(state - 1)
  },
```

To help keep your ReasonReact apps ready for the coming ReactJS Fiber release, ensure that everything in `reducer` is pure. One way to trigger side effects indirectly while keeping `reducer` pure is by using `ReasonReact.UpdateWithSideEffects`:

```
reducer: (action, state) =>
  switch (action) {
  | Increment =>
    ReasonReact.UpdateWithSideEffects(
      state + 1,
      (_self => Js.log("incremented")),
    )
  | Decrement => ReasonReact.Update(state - 1)
  },
```

The return value of `reducer` must be one of the following variant constructors:

- `ReasonReact.NoUpdate`
- `ReasonReact.Update(state)`
- `ReasonReact.SideEffects(self => unit)`
- `ReasonReact.UpdateWithSideEffects(state, self => unit)`

We can trigger new actions from within our side effects, since we're again provided with `self`:

```
reducer: (action, state) =>
  switch (action) {
  | Increment =>
    ReasonReact.UpdateWithSideEffects(
      state + 1,
```

```
    (
      self =>
        Js.Global.setTimeout(() => self.send(Decrement), 1000) |> ignore
    ),
  )
| Decrement => ReasonReact.Update(state - 1)
},
```

After incrementing, the `reducer` triggers a side-effect that triggers the `Decrement` action after one second.

Refactoring

Let's imagine we now need our stateful component to display a message that congratulates the user when they get to a count of 10, and once the message is displayed, the user can close the message by clicking a close button. Thanks to our helpful compiler, we can follow these steps:

1. Update the shape of `state`
2. Update the available `actions`
3. Step through the compiler errors
4. Update the `render` function

The compiler messages will remind us to update the component's initial state and reducer. Since we now need to also keep track of whether or not to display a message, let's change the shape of `state` to this:

```
type state = {
  count: int,
  showMessage: bool
};
```

For our actions, let's combine `Increment` and `Decrement` into one constructor that accepts an `int`, and we'll have a new constructor to toggle the message:

```
type action =
  | UpdateCount(int)
  | ToggleMessage;
```

Now, instead of `Increment` and `Decrement`, we have `UpdateCount`, which holds an integer representing the amount to change the current count by.

Creating ReasonReact Components

After compiling, we see a friendly error letting us know that our previous action `Decrement` cannot be found:

```
We've found a bug for you!
24 | render: self =>
25 |   <>
26 |     <button onClick={_event => self.send(Decrement)}>
27 |       {ReasonReact.string("-")}
28 |     </button>
The variant constructor Decrement can't be found.
- If it's defined in another module or file, bring it into scope by:
- Annotating it with said module name: let food = MyModule.Apple
- Or specifying its type: let food: MyModule.fruit = Apple
- Constructors and modules are both capitalized. Did you want the latter?
Then instead of let foo = Bar, try module Foo = Bar.
```

In the `render` function, replace `Increment` with `UpdateCount(+1)` and `Decrement` with `UpdateCount(-1)`:

```
render: self =>
  <>
    <button onClick={_event => self.send(UpdateCount(-1))}>
      {ReasonReact.string("-")}
    </button>
    <span> {ReasonReact.string(string_of_int(self.state))} </span>
    <button onClick={_event => self.send(UpdateCount(1))}>
      {ReasonReact.string("+")}
    </button>
  </>,
```

Compiling again, we're informed that in our reducer, `Increment` does not belong to type `action`. Let's update our reducer to handle both `UpdateCount` and `ToggleMessage`. If we were to forget a constructor, the compiler would let us know that the switch expression in the reducer is not exhaustive:

```
reducer: (action, state) =>
  switch (action) {
  | UpdateCount(delta) =>
    let count = state.count + delta;
    ReasonReact.UpdateWithSideEffects(
      {...state, count},
      (
        self =>
          if (count == 10) {
            self.send(ToggleMessage);
          }
      ),
```

```
    );
| ToggleMessage =>
  ReasonReact.Update({...state, showMessage: !state.showMessage})
},
```

There are few things to mention regarding the preceding code snippet:

- In `UpdateCount`, we're declaring a binding `count` that reflects the new count.
- We're using `...` to override just a portion of the state record.
- Thanks to record punning support, we can write `{...state, count}` instead of `{...state, count: count}`.
- `UpdateCount` is using `UpdateWithSideEffects` to trigger a `ToggleMessage` action when the count reaches 10; we could have instead done this:

```
| UpdateCount(delta) =>
  let count = state.count + delta;
  ReasonReact.Update(
    if (count == 10) {
      {count, showMessage: true};
    } else {
      {...state, count};
    },
  );
```

I prefer using `UpdateWithSideEffects` so that `UpdateCount` only ever has to worry about its count field, and if some other field needs to get updated, `UpdateCount` can trigger the right action for that to happen, without needing to know how it needs to happen.

After compiling here, we get an interesting compiler error:

```
We've found a bug for you!

16 | switch (action) {
17 | | UpdateCount(delta) =>
18 | let count = state.count + delta;
19 | ReasonReact.UpdateWithSideEffects(
20 | {...state, count},

This has type:
  int
But somewhere wanted:
  state
```

Creating ReasonReact Components

The compiler sees `state` in `state.count` on line 18 (shown previously) as having type `int` instead of type `state`. This is because our render function is using `string_of_int(self.state)` instead of `string_of_int(self.state.count)`. After updating our render function to reflect this, we get another similar message complaining that type `int` and type `state` are incompatible. That's because our initial state is still returning `0` instead of a record of type `state`.

After updating initial state, the code finally compiles successfully:

```
initialState: () => {count: 0, showMessage: false},
```

Now, we're ready to update the render function to display a message when the count reaches 10:

```
render: self =>
  <>
    <button onClick={_event => self.send(UpdateCount(-1))}>
      {ReasonReact.string("-")}
    </button>
    <span> {ReasonReact.string(string_of_int(self.state.count))} </span>
    <button onClick={_event => self.send(UpdateCount(1))}>
      {ReasonReact.string("+")}
    </button>
    {
      if (self.state.showMessage) {
        <>
          <p>
            {ReasonReact.string("Congratulations! You've reached ten!")}
          </p>
          <button onClick={_event => self.send(ToggleMessage)}>
            {ReasonReact.string("close")}
          </button>
        </>;
      } else {
        ReasonReact.null;
      }
    }
  </>,
```

Since `if/else` is an expression in Reason, we can use it within JSX to either render markup or `ReasonReact.null` (which has type `ReasonReact.reactElement`).

[54]

Instance variables

Although our example correctly shows the message when count reaches 10 for the first time, there is nothing preventing our `ToggleMessage` action from getting fired again within the `UpdateCount` case in the reducer. If a user gets to 10, then decrements and then increments, the message is toggled again. To ensure that `UpdateCount` only ever triggers the `ToggleMessage` action once, we can use an **instance variable** in state.

In ReactJS, every time something in state changes, the component gets re-rendered. In ReasonReact, instance variables never trigger a re-render, and can be correctly placed within a component's state.

Let's add an instance variable to keep track of whether the user has already seen the message:

```
type state = {
  count: int,
  showMessage: bool,
  userHasSeenMessage: ref(bool)
};
```

Ref and mutable records

The difference between ReasonReact instance variables and normal state variables is the use of `ref`. Previously, we saw that `state.userHasSeenMessage` is of type `ref(bool)` instead of `bool`. That makes `state.userHasSeenMessage` an instance variable.

Since `ref` is just syntactic sugar for a record type with a mutable field, let's first discuss mutable record fields.

To allow a record field to be mutable, prefix the field's name with `mutable`. Then, those fields can be updated in place using the = operator:

```
type ref('a) = {
  mutable contents: 'a
};

let foo = {contents: 5};
Js.log(foo.contents); /* 5 */
foo.contents = 6;
Js.log(foo.contents); /* 6 */
```

However, the type declaration is already included in Reason's standard library, so we can omit it, and the rest of the preceding code would still work, declaring it shadowed the original type declaration. We can prove this by shadowing the `ref` type with an immutable record:

```
type ref('a) = {contents: 'a};

let foo = {contents: 5};
Js.log(foo.contents); /* 5 */
foo.contents = 6;
Js.log(foo.contents); /* 6 */
```

The compiler fails with the following error:

```
We've found a bug for you!

The record field contents is not mutable
```

In addition to having a built-in type definition, `ref` also has some built-in functions. Namely, `ref` is used to create a record of type `ref`, and `^` is used to get the contents of a `ref`, and `:=` is used to set the contents of a ref:

```
type foo = ref(int);

let foo = ref(5);
Js.log(foo^); /* 5 */
foo := 6;
Js.log(foo^); /* 6 */
```

Let's go back to our ReasonReact example, and let's use our new `userHasSeenMessage` instance variable. After updating the shape of our state, we need to also update the component's initial state:

```
initialState: () => {
  count: 0,
  showMessage: false,
  userHasSeenMessage: ref(false),
},
```

Now, our code again compiles, and we can update `reducer` to use this instance variable:

```
reducer: (action, state) =>
  switch (action) {
  | UpdateCount(delta) =>
    let count = state.count + delta;
    if (! state.userHasSeenMessage^ && count == 10) {
      state.userHasSeenMessage := true;
```

```
      ReasonReact.UpdateWithSideEffects(
        {...state, count},
        (self => self.send(ToggleMessage)),
      );
    } else {
      ReasonReact.Update({...state, count});
    };
  | ToggleMessage =>
    ReasonReact.Update({...state, showMessage: !state.showMessage})
  },
```

Now, the message is correctly displayed once and only once.

Navigation menu

Let's use what we've learned so far as a foundation to build upon while creating an application with a navigation menu and client-side routing. On touch devices, users will be able to swipe to close the menu, and the menu will respond in real time to the user's touch. If the user swipes the menu when it's more than 50% closed and then releases, the menu will close; otherwise, it will remain open. The one exception is if the user swipes the menu closed with a high enough velocity; it will always close.

We will be working with this application throughout the rest of the book. To follow along, clone the GitHub repo and navigate to the directory representing the start of this chapter:

```
git clone https://github.com/PacktPublishing/ReasonML-Quick-Start-Guide.git
cd ReasonML-Quick-Start-Guide
cd Chapter03/app-start
npm install
```

Let's take a moment to see what we have to work with. You will see the following directory structure:

```
├── bsconfig.json
├── package-lock.json
├── package.json
├── src
│   ├── App.re
│   ├── App.scss
│   ├── Index.re
│   ├── Index.scss
│   ├── img
│   │   └── icon
│   │       ├── arrow.svg
│   │       ├── chevron.svg
```

Creating ReasonReact Components

```
|   |       └── hamburger.svg
|   └── index.html
└── webpack.config.js
```

Our `bsconfig.json` is set up to place compiled `.bs.js` files within `lib/es6/src`, and we've configured webpack to look for `lib/es6/src/Index.bs.js` as an entry point.

Run `npm install` and then `npm start` to serve our app at `http://localhost:3000` with both bsb and webpack in watch mode.

Currently, our app displays a blue navigation bar with a hamburger icon. Clicking on the icon opens a menu and clicking outside the menu closes it.

In `App.re`, our state is currently a single field record that keeps track of the menu's state:

```
type state = {isOpen: bool};
```

We have one action:

```
type action =
  | ToggleMenu(bool);
```

And our reducer takes care of updating the menu's state:

```
reducer: (action, _state) =>
  switch (action) {
  | ToggleMenu(isOpen) => ReasonReact.Update({isOpen: isOpen})
  },
```

> Although Reason supports record punning, it does not work for single field records, since Reason treats `{isOpen}` as a block instead of a record.

Our render function renders a `<div />` element with a conditional class name depending on the current state:

```
<div
  className={"App" ++ (self.state.isOpen ? " overlay" : "")}
  onClick={
    _event =>
      if (self.state.isOpen) {
        self.send(ToggleMenu(false));
      }
  }>
```

[58]

`App.scss` uses the `overlay` class to display a dark overlay behind the navigation menu only when it's open:

```
.App {
  min-height: 100vh;

  &:after {
    content: "";
    transition: opacity 450ms cubic-bezier(0.23, 1, 0.32, 1),
      transform 0ms cubic-bezier(0.23, 1, 0.32, 1) 450ms;
    position: fixed;
    top: 0;
    right: 0;
    bottom: 0;
    left: 0;
    background-color: rgba(0, 0, 0, 0.33);
    transform: translateX(-100%);
    opacity: 0;
    z-index: 1;
  }

  &.overlay {
    &:after {
      transition: opacity 450ms cubic-bezier(0.23, 1, 0.32, 1);
      transform: translateX(0%);
      opacity: 1;
    }
  }
  ...
}
```

Notice how the `transition` property is defined for both `.App:after` and `.App.overly:after`, the former includes a transition on the `transform` property with a `450ms` delay while the latter removes that transition. This has the effect of allowing a smooth transition even when the menu is closed.

Bindings

Let's inspect the binding to JavaScript's `require` function at the top of `App.re`. Since we're going to dive deeper into BuckleScript in `Chapter 4`, *BuckleScript, Belt, and Interoperability*, let's defer discussing the details and just briefly see what this binding is doing:

```
[@bs.val] external require: string => string = "";

require("../../../src/App.scss");
```

The `external` keyword creates a new binding, similar to the `let` keyword. After binding to JavaScript's `require` function, we can use it in Reason, as long as we're using the BuckleScript compiler. We use it to require `App.scss` as well as a few images. Inspecting the compiled output at `lib/es6/src/App.bs.js` shows that the preceding Reason code compiles to the following:

```
require("../../../src/App.scss");
```

Webpack handles the rest from there.

Events

Since the top-level `<div />` element has a click event handler that always closes the menu, any clicks on its children also fire that top-level click event handler. To allow the menu to open (or remain open), we need to call `event.stopPropagation()` on click events for some of its child elements.

In ReasonReact, we can do this with the `ReactEvent` module:

```
onClick=(event => ReactEvent.Mouse.stopPropagation(event))
```

The `ReactEvent` module has submodules corresponding to each of ReactJS's synthetic events:

- Clipboard events
- Composition events
- Keyboard events
- Focus events
- Form events
- Mouse events
- Pointer events
- Selection events
- Touch events
- UI events
- Wheel events
- Media events
- Image events
- Animation events
- Transition events

For more information on ReactJS's synthetic events, visit `https://reactjs.org/docs/events.html`.

To get values such as `event.changedTouches.item(0).clientX` from a touch event, we use a combination of ReasonReact and BuckleScript.

Js.t Object

BuckleScript allows us to access arbitrary JavaScript object fields using the `##` syntax. We can use syntax on any `Js.t` type, which is a Reason type for arbitrary JavaScript objects. We'll learn more about this and other interoperability features in Chapter 4, *BuckleScript, Belt, and Interoperability*.

Since `ReactEvent.Touch.changedTouches(event)` returns a plain old JavaScript object, we can access its fields using the following:

```
/* App.re */
ReactEvent.Touch.changedTouches(event)##item(0)##clientX
```

Looking in the compiled output, we see that it is what we want:

```
/* App.bs.js */
event.changedTouches.item(0).clientX
```

We'll use this to add the touch feature to our menu so that users can swipe the menu closed and see the menu move as they swipe.

Adding actions

Let's start by adding actions for `TouchStart`, `TouchMove`, and `TouchEnd`:

```
type action =
  | ToggleMenu(bool)
  | TouchStart(float)
  | TouchMove(float)
  | TouchEnd;
```

We'll need the touch event's `clientX` property only for `TouchStart` and `TouchMove`.

Let's add the event listeners on the top-level `<div />` component:

```
render: self =>
  <div
```

Creating ReasonReact Components

```
          className={"App" ++ (self.state.isOpen ? " overlay" : "")}
          onClick={
            _event =>
              if (self.state.isOpen) {
                self.send(ToggleMenu(false));
              }
          }
          onTouchStart={
            event =>
              self.send(
                TouchStart(
                  ReactEvent.Touch.changedTouches(event)##item(0)##clientX,
                ),
              )
          }
          onTouchMove={
            event =>
              self.send(
                TouchMove(
                  ReactEvent.Touch.changedTouches(event)##item(0)##clientX,
                ),
              )
          }
          onTouchEnd={_event => self.send(TouchEnd) }>
```

In our reducer, let's just log those `clientX` values for now:

```
reducer: (action, state) =>
  switch (action) {
  | ToggleMenu(isOpen) => ReasonReact.Update({isOpen: isOpen})
  | TouchStart(clientX) =>
    Js.log2("Start", clientX);
    ReasonReact.NoUpdate;
  | TouchMove(clientX) =>
    Js.log2("Move", clientX);
    ReasonReact.NoUpdate;
  | TouchEnd =>
    Js.log("End");
    ReasonReact.NoUpdate;
  },
```

To figure out the overall direction of a user's swipe, we need the first and last `clientX` values for that swipe. The menu should move in proportion to the difference of the first and last `clientX` values, but only if the user is swiping in the direction that would close the menu.

Our state now includes a `touches` record that holds the value for the first and last `clientX` values:

```
type touches = {
  first: option(float),
  last: option(float),
};

type state = {
  isOpen: bool,
  touches,
};
```

Since we cannot nest record type definitions, we define the `touches` type separately and include it in `state`. You'll notice `state.touches.first` is of type `option(float)` because it's possible that the user isn't using a touch device or that the user hasn't yet interacted.

Changing the shape of our state requires us to also change the initial state:

```
initialState: () => {
  isOpen: false,
  touches: {
    first: None,
    last: None,
  },
},
```

In the reducer, if the menu is open, we update `state.touches` with a fresh new record in the `TouchStart` case, but in the `TouchMove` case, we only update `state.touches.last`. If the menu is not currently open, `ReasonReact.NoUpdate` is returned:

```
reducer: (action, state) =>
  switch (action) {
  | ToggleMenu(isOpen) => ReasonReact.Update({...state, isOpen})
  | TouchStart(clientX) =>
    if (state.isOpen) {
      ReasonReact.Update({
        ...state,
        touches: {
          first: Some(clientX),
          last: None,
        },
      });
    } else {
      ReasonReact.NoUpdate;
    }
```

Creating ReasonReact Components

```
    | TouchMove(clientX) =>
      if (state.isOpen) {
        ReasonReact.Update({
          ...state,
          touches: {
            ...state.touches,
            last: Some(clientX),
          },
        });
      } else {
        ReasonReact.NoUpdate;
      }
    | TouchEnd => ReasonReact.NoUpdate
    },
```

We'll soon use this state to conditionally set an inline style on the `<nav />` element.

Inline styles

In ReasonReact, we can add inline styles via `ReactDOMRe.Style.make`, which accepts CSS properties as optional labelled arguments. Since they are all optional, passing `unit` is necessary to call the function:

```
style={ReactDOMRe.Style.make(~backgroundColor="yellow", ())}
```

Applying this to our `<nav />` element, we can conditionally add a style if we have both a first and last touch in state:

```
style={
  switch (self.state.touches) {
  | {first: Some(x), last: Some(x')} =>
    ReactDOMRe.Style.make(
      ~transform=
        "translateX("
        ++ string_of_float(x' -. x > 0.0 ? 0.0 : x' -. x)
        ++ "0px)",
      ~transition="none",
      (),
    )
  | _ => ReactDOMRe.Style.make()
  }
}
```

Within the `transform` property, we concatenate with `"0px"` instead of just `"px"` since the `float` type always includes a decimal point, but it's possible that the user swipes a distance of exactly one hundred pixels, and `transform: translateX(100.px)` is not valid CSS, but `transform: translateX(100.0px)` is.

Running this on a touch device shows that we're able to get the menu's position to change based on the user's swipe. Now, let's focus on the `TouchEnd` case within the reducer. For now, let's set the menu to remain open if the user swipes the menu less than half way closed, and close it otherwise. If `state.touches.last` is `None`, then the user did not swipe, and we don't update `state`:

```
| TouchEnd =>
  if (state.isOpen) {
    let x = Belt.Option.getWithDefault(state.touches.last, 0.0);
    if (x < 300.0 /. 2.0) {
      ReasonReact.UpdateWithSideEffects(
        {
          ...state,
          touches: {
            first: None,
            last: None,
          },
        },
        (self => self.send(ToggleMenu(false))),
      );
    } else {
      ReasonReact.Update({
        ...state,
        touches: {
          first: None,
          last: None,
        },
      });
    };
  } else {
    ReasonReact.NoUpdate;
  }
```

Notice that we reset `state.touches` to a fresh new record with `{first: None, last: None}`, which results in an empty style prop on the `<nav />` element.

This current implementation assumes that the width of the navigation is `300px`. Instead of assuming, we can use a React ref to get a reference to the DOM node, and then get its `clientWidth`.

React ref

The React ref is just an instance variable of `state`:

```
type state = {
  isOpen: bool,
  touches,
  width: ref(float),
};
```

We attach the React ref on the `<nav />` element by setting the `ref` property to the result of `self.handle((ref, self) => ...)`:

```
ref={
  self.handle((ref, self) =>
    self.state.width :=
      (
        switch (Js.Nullable.toOption(ref)) {
        | None => 0.0
        | Some(r) => ReactDOMRe.domElementToObj(r)##clientWidth
        }
      )
  )
}
```

Since a React ref could be `null` in JavaScript, we convert it to an option and pattern match on its value.

The type of the React ref depends on whether it is a DOM element or a React component. The former's type is `Dom.element`, and the latter's is `ReasonReact.reactRef`. To convert a `ReasonReact.reactRef` to a JavaScript object, use `ReasonReact.refToJsObj` instead of `ReactDOMRe.domElementToObj`.

Then, in the reducer, we can use `state.width` instead of `300.0` as the menu's width. Since the `TouchStart` and `TouchMove` actions always update state when the menu is open, the `<App />` component is always re-rendered, which causes our React ref function to re-run, and we can be reasonably sure that the menu's width is always correct.

Velocity

To get the velocity of a user's swipe, we'll need to also store the current time along with the touch event's `clientX`. Let's bind to the browser's `performance.now()` method:

```
[@bs.val] [@bs.scope "performance"] external now: unit => float = "";
```

And we'll make some room for the touch's current time in the `touches` type:

```
type touches = {
  first: option((float, float)),
  last: option((float, float)),
};
```

In the reducer, we then change `Some(clientX)` to `Some((clientX, now()))`.

Now, we can calculate the velocity of a user's swipe in the `TouchEnd` case:

```
| TouchEnd =>
  if (state.isOpen) {
    let (x, t) =
      Belt.Option.getWithDefault(state.touches.first, (0.0, 0.0));
    let (x', t') =
      Belt.Option.getWithDefault(state.touches.last, (0.0, 0.0));
    let velocity = (x' -. x) /. (t' -. t);
    let state = {
      ...state,
      touches: {
        first: None,
        last: None,
      },
    };
    if (velocity < (-0.3) || x' < state.width^ /. 2.0) {
      ReasonReact.UpdateWithSideEffects(
        state,
        (self => self.send(ToggleMenu(false))),
      );
    } else {
      ReasonReact.Update(state);
    };
  } else {
    ReasonReact.NoUpdate;
  }
```

A velocity of -0.3 pixels per millisecond feels right to me, but feel free to use whatever feels right for you.

Notice how we can use pattern matching to destructure (x, t), which creates two bindings in scope. Also, x' is a valid name for a binding in Reason and is commonly pronounced *x prime*. Lastly, notice how our state is shadowed to prevent writing duplicate code.

To finish the velocity feature, we update the style property in the render function to treat both state.touches.first and state.touches.last as tuples:

```
style=(
  switch (self.state.touches) {
  | {first: Some((x, _)), last: Some((x', _))} =>
    ReactDOMRe.Style.make(
      ~transform=
        "translateX("
        ++ string_of_float(x' -. x > 0.0 ? 0.0 : x' -. x)
        ++ "0px)",
      ~transition="none",
      (),
    )
  | _ => ReactDOMRe.Style.make()
  }
)
```

Now, when open, the menu responds nicely to a touch—super cool!

Client-side routing

ReasonReact comes with a built-in router found in the ReasonReact.Router module. It is quite unopinionated and therefore flexible. The public API has only four functions:

- ReasonReact.Router.watchUrl: (url => unit) => watcherID
- ReasonReact.Router.unwatchUrl: watcherID => unit
- ReasonReact.Router.push: string => unit
- ReasonReact.Router.dangerouslyGetInitialUrl: unit => url

The watchUrl function starts watching the URL for changes. When changed, the url => unit callback is called. The unwatchUrl function stops watching the URL.

The push function sets the URL, and the dangerouslyGetInitialUrl function gets a record of type url. The dangerouslyGetInitialUrl function is meant to be used only within the didMount lifecycle hook, alongside watchUrl, to prevent issues with stale information.

The `url` type is defined as follows:

```
type url = {
  path: list(string),
  hash: string,
  search: string,
};
```

We'll learn more about the `list` type constructor in Chapter 4, *BuckleScript, Belt, and Interoperability*. The `path` field in the `url` record is of type `list(string)`. If the value of `window.location.pathname` is `"/book/title/edit"`, the value of `url.path` will be `["book", "title", "edit"]`, which is a list of strings. The syntax makes it look like a JavaScript array, but there are some differences. Briefly, Reason lists are singly linked lists that are immutable and homogeneous, meaning all elements must be of the same type.

The `watcherID` type is an **abstract type**. We'll learn more about abstract types in Chapter 6, *CSS-in-JS (in Reason)*. The only way to get a value of type `watcherID` is as the return value of `ReasonReact.Router.watchUrl`.

Let's create a router component that wraps our `<App />` component and provides it with a `currentRoute` prop. What follows was inspired by an example from Khoa Nguyen (@thangngoc89).

First, let's create placeholder components for `<Home />`, `<Page1 />`, `<Page2 />`, and `<Page3 />`. Then, within `Router.re`, let's create a type that represents a route along with a list of routes:

```
type route = {
  href: string,
  title: string,
  component: ReasonReact.reactElement,
};

let routes = [
  {href: "/", title: "Home", component: <Home />},
  {href: "/page1", title: "Page1", component: <Page1 />},
  {href: "/page2", title: "Page2", component: <Page2 />},
  {href: "/page3", title: "Page3", component: <Page3 />},
];
```

Each route has an `href`, `title`, and an associated `component`, which will be rendered within `<App />` if that route is the current route.

Current route

In `Index.re`, let's wrap `<App />` within a router component that provides the `currentRoute` prop:

```
ReactDOMRe.renderToElementWithId(
  <Router.WithRouter>
    ...((~currentRoute) => <App currentRoute />)
  </Router.WithRouter>,
  "root",
);
```

In `Router.re`, we define three components—`<WithRouter />`, `<Link />`, and `<NavLink />`—using the `module` syntax. Since each file is also a module, those three components are nested under the `Router` module, and in `Index.re` we need to tell the compiler to look for `<WithRouter />` within the `Router` module:

```
module WithRouter = {
  type state = route;
  type action =
    | ChangeRoute(route);
  let component = ReasonReact.reducerComponent("WithRouter");
  let make = children => {
    ...component,
    didMount: self => {
      let watcherID =
        ReasonReact.Router.watchUrl(url =>
          self.send(ChangeRoute(urlToRoute(url)))
        );
      ();
      self.onUnmount(() => ReasonReact.Router.unwatchUrl(watcherID));
    },
    initialState: () =>
      urlToRoute(ReasonReact.Router.dangerouslyGetInitialUrl()),
    reducer: (action, _state) =>
      switch (action) {
      | ChangeRoute(route) => ReasonReact.Update(route)
      },
    render: self => children(~currentRoute=self.state),
  };
};
```

We've seen all of these concepts before. `<WithRouter />` is just a reducer component. The component's state is the same route type defined earlier and there is only one action to change the route. Once `<WithRouter />` is mounted, `ReasonReact.Router` begins watching the URL, and whenever it changes, the `ChangeRoute` action is triggered, which calls the reducer, which then updates state, which then re-renders `<App />` with an updated `currentRoute` prop.

To ensure that our menu closes whenever `<App />` receives a fresh `currentRoute` prop, we add a `willReceiveProps` lifecycle hook for `<App />`:

```
willReceiveProps: self => {...self.state, isOpen: false},
```

Helper functions

Since `url.path` of `ReasonReact.Router` is a list of strings, and our `Router.route.href` is a string, we need a way to convert from string to a list of strings:

```
let hrefToPath = href =>
  Js.String.replaceByRe([%bs.re "/(^\\/)|(\\/$)/"], "", href)
  |> Js.String.split("/")
  |> Belt.List.fromArray;
```

> We'll discuss Reason's pipe operator (`|>`) and JavaScript interoperability in Chapter 4, *BuckleScript, Belt, and Interoperability*.

We also need a way to convert a `url` to a `route` for use in initial state, as well as within the callback function of `watchUrl`:

```
let urlToRoute = (url: ReasonReact.Router.url) =>
  switch (
    Belt.List.getBy(routes, route => url.path == hrefToPath(route.href))
  ) {
  | None => Belt.List.headExn(routes)
  | Some(route) => route
  };
```

In Chapter 4, *BuckleScript, Belt, and Interoperability*, we will dive deeper into BuckleScript, Belt, and JavaScript interoperability. The `urlToRoute` function tries to find a `route` within the `routes` list whose `url.path` is structurally equal to `route.href` after it's converted to a list of strings.

If no such `route` exists, it returns the first `route` from the `routes` list, which is the one associated with the `<Home />` component. Otherwise, the matching `route` is returned.

The `<Link />` component is a simple stateless component that renders an anchor link. Note how the click handler prevents the default browser behavior and updates the URL:

```
module Link = {
  let component = ReasonReact.statelessComponent("Link");
  let make = (~href, ~className="", children) => {
    ...component,
    render: self =>
      <a
        href
        className
        onClick=(
          self.handle((event, _self) => {
            ReactEvent.Mouse.preventDefault(event);
            ReasonReact.Router.push(href);
          })
        )>
        ...children
      </a>,
  };
};
```

The `<NavLink />` component wraps the `<Link />` component, and is provided with the current route as a prop that it uses to conditionally set an `active` class:

```
module NavLink = {
  let component = ReasonReact.statelessComponent("NavLink");
  let make = (~href, children) => {
    ...component,
    render: _self =>
      <WithRouter>
        ...(
          (~currentRoute) =>
            <Link
              href className=(currentRoute.href == href ? "active" : "")>
              ...children
            </Link>
        )
      </WithRouter>,
  };
};
```

Usage

Now that we've defined the router, we can rewrite our navigation menu links to use the `<NavLink />` component instead of the raw anchor link directly:

```
<li>
  <Router.NavLink href="/">
    (ReasonReact.string("Home"))
  </Router.NavLink>
</li>
```

Wherever we want to display the current page's title, we can simply access the `title` field on the current route:

```
<h1> (ReasonReact.string(currentRoute.title)) </h1>
```

And, we can render a route's associated component in a similar way:

```
<main> currentRoute.component </main>
```

It's important to emphasize that ReasonReact's router does not dictate what the callback of `watchUrl` should do. In our case, we trigger an action that updates the current route, which is just an arbitrary record. It's completely reasonable for the route type to be something entirely different. Also, there is no law that says the router should be the top-level component. There is a lot of room for creativity here and I'm personally excited to see what the community comes up with.

Summary

In this chapter, we saw how ReasonReact is a simpler, safer way to build React components. Having Reason's type system enforcing correct component usage at compile time is a huge win. Also, it makes refactoring safer, cheaper, and a much more pleasant experience. ReasonReact is *just* Reason, much like how ReactJS is *just* JavaScript. All of what we've done so far is just Reason and ReasonReact without any third-party libraries such as Redux or React Router.

As we'll see in `Chapter 4`, *BuckleScript, Belt, and Interoperability*, we also have the option to use existing JavaScript (and ReactJS) solutions within Reason. After getting more comfortable with BuckleScript, the Belt standard library, and JavaScript interoperability, we'll add route transitions.

4
BuckleScript, Belt, and Interoperability

In this chapter, we'll take a closer look at the BuckleScript-specific features that are available to us. We'll also learn about recursion and recursive data structures. By the end of this chapter, we'll have come full circle in the introduction to Reason and its ecosystem. In doing so, we'll have done the following:

- Learned more about Reason's module system
- Explored more of Reason's primitive data structures (arrays and lists)
- Seen how the various pipe operators can make code more readable
- Become familiar with the Reason and Belt standard libraries
- Created bindings to a JavaScript module for use within Reason
- Added route transitions to our application by binding to React Transition Group components

To follow along, use any environment you wish. Much of what we'll be doing is not ReasonReact-specific. Toward the end of the chapter, we'll resume building our ReasonReact app.

Module scope

As you now know, all `.re` files are modules and all modules are globally available—including nested ones. By default, all types and bindings can be accessed from anywhere by providing the namespace. However, doing this over and over quickly becomes tedious. Luckily, we have a few ways to make this more pleasant:

```
/* Foo.re */
type fromFoo =
  | Add(int, int)
  | Multiply(int, int);
```

```
let a = 1;
let b = 2;
```

Next, we'll use the `Foo` module's `fromFoo` type along with it's bindings within another module in different ways:

- **Option 1**: Without any sugar:

    ```
    /* Bar.re */
    let fromFoo = Foo.Add(Foo.a, Foo.b);
    ```

- **Option 2**: Alias the module to a shorter name. For example, we can declare a new module `F` and bind it to the existing module `Foo`:

    ```
    /* Bar.re */
    module F = Foo;
    let fromFoo = F.Add(F.a, F.b);
    ```

- **Option 3**: Locally open the module using the `Module.()` syntax. This syntax only works with a single expression:

    ```
    /* Bar.re */
    let fromFoo = Foo.(Add(a, b));
    ```

- **Option 4**: In the OOP sense, have `Bar` extend `Foo` using `include`:

    ```
    /* Bar.re */
    include Foo;
    let a = 4; /* override Foo.a */
    let fromFoo = Add(a, b);
    ```

- **Option 5**: Globally `open` the module. Use `open` sparingly in large scopes, since it becomes hard to know which types and bindings belong to which modules:

    ```
    /* Bar.re */
    open Foo;
    let fromFoo = Add(a, b);
    ```

Prefer using `open` in local scopes:

```
/* Bar.re */
let fromFoo = {
  open Foo;
  Add(a, b);
};
```

The preceding syntax will reformat (via `refmt`) to Option 3's syntax, but remember that Option 3's syntax only works with single expressions. For example, the following isn't able to be converted into Option 3's syntax:

```
/* Bar.re */
let fromFoo = {
  open Foo;
  Js.log("foo");
  let result = Add(a, b);
};
```

The Reason standard library is found within a variety of modules that are already available to us. For example, Reason's standard library includes an `Array` module, and we can access its functions using the dot notation (that is, `Array.length`).

In Chapter 5, *Effective ML*, we'll learn how to hide a module's types and bindings so that they aren't globally available if we don't want them to be.

Data structures

We've already seen several of Reason's primitive data structures including strings, integers, floats, tuples, records, and variants. Let's explore a few more.

Array

Reason arrays compile to regular JavaScript arrays. Reason arrays are as follows:

- Homogeneous (all elements must be of the same type)
- Mutable
- Fast at random access and updates

They look like this:

```
let array = [|"first", "second", "third"|];
```

Accessing and updating elements of an array are the same as in JavaScript:

```
array[0] = "updated";
```

In JavaScript, we map over the array, as follows:

```
/* JavaScript */
array.map(e => e + "-mapped")
```

To do the same in Reason, we have a few different options.

Using the Reason standard library

The Reason standard library's `Array` module contains several functions, but not all the ones you'd expect coming from JavaScript. It does have a `map` function, however:

```
/* Reason standard library */
let array = [|"first", "second", "third"|];
Array.map(e => e ++ "-mapped", array);
```

The type of `Array.map` is as follows:

```
('a => 'b, array('a)) => array('b);
```

The type signature says `map` accepts a function of type `'a => 'b`, an array of type `'a`, and returns an array of type `'b`. Note that, `'a` and `'b` are **type variables**. Type variables are like normal variables, except for types. In the preceding example, `map` has a type:

```
(string => string, array(string)) => array(string);
```

This is because the `'a` and `'b` type variables were both consistently replaced with the concrete `string` type.

Note that, when using `Array.map`, the compiled output does not compile to JavaScript's `Array.prototype.map`—it has its own implementation:

```
/* in the compiled output */
...
require("./stdlib/array.js");
...
```

> The Reason standard library documentation can be found here:
>
> https://reasonml.github.io/api

Using the Belt standard library

The Reason standard library is actually the OCaml standard library. It was not created with JavaScript in mind. The Belt standard library was created by the same person who created BuckleScript—Hongbo Zhang—and ships with BuckleScript. Belt was made with JavaScript in mind and is especially known for its performance. The Belt standard library is accessed via the `Belt` module:

```
/* Belt standard library */
let array = [|"first", "second", "third"|];
Belt.Array.map(array, e => e ++ "-mapped");
```

> The Belt standard library documentation can be found here:
>
> https://bucklescript.github.io/bucklescript/api/Belt.html

Using BuckleScript's built-in JavaScript bindings

Another great option is to use BuckleScript's built-in JavaScript bindings, found in the `Js` module:

```
/* BuckleScript's JavaScript bindings */
let array = [|"first", "second", "third"|];
Js.Array.map(e => e ++ "-mapped", array);
```

This option has the advantage of not requiring any dependencies in the compiled output. It also has a very familiar API. However, since not all Reason data structures exist in JavaScript, you'll likely be using a standard library. If so, prefer Belt.

> BuckleScript's binding documentation can be found here:
>
> https://bucklescript.github.io/bucklescript/api/Js.html

Using a custom binding

There's nothing stopping you from writing your own custom bindings:

```
[@bs.send] external map: (array('a), 'a => 'b) => array('b) = "";
let array = [|"first", "second", "third"|];
map(array, e => e ++ "-mapped")
```

Of course, you should favor using the built-in bindings in the Js module instead. We'll explore more custom bindings later in this chapter.

Using raw JavaScript

A last-resort option is to use actual JavaScript within Reason:

```
let array = [|"first", "second", "third"|];
let map = [%raw {|
  function(f, array) {
    return array.map(f)
  }
|}];
map(e => e ++ "-mapped", array)
```

BuckleScript lets us drop into raw JavaScript as a way to stay productive while we're learning. Of course, when doing this, we give up the safety that Reason provides us with. So, once you are ready, convert any raw JavaScript code back into more idiomatic Reason.

When it comes to using raw JavaScript, use % for expressions and %% for statements. Remember, the {| |} is Reason's multiline string syntax:

```
let array = [%raw "['first', 'second', 'third']"];
[%%raw {|
  array = array.map(e => e + "-mapped");
|}];
```

Using the raw expression syntax, we're also able to annotate types:

```
let array: array(string) = [%raw "['first', 'second', 'third']"];
```

We can even annotate function types:

```
let random: unit => float = [%raw
  {|
    function() {
      return Math.random();
    }
  |}
];
```

Although arrays are familiar when coming from JavaScript, you'll likely find yourself using lists instead, as they are ubiquitous in functional programming. Lists are both immutable and recursive. Let's now see how to use this recursive data structure.

List

Reason lists are as follows:

- Homogeneous
- Immutable
- Fast at prepending and accessing the head of the list

They look like this:

```
let list = ["first", "second", "third"];
```

The head of the list, in this case, is `"first"`. By now, we've seen that it's not difficult to work with immutable data structures. Instead of mutation, we create updated copies.

When working with lists, we can't use JavaScript bindings directly, since lists do not exist in JavaScript as a primitive data structure. However, we can convert lists to arrays and vice versa:

```
/* Belt standard library */
let list = ["first", "second", "third"];
let array = Belt.List.toArray(list);

let array = [|"first", "second", "third"|];
let list = Belt.List.fromArray(array);

/* Reason standard library */
let list = ["first", "second", "third"];
let array = Array.of_list(list);

let array = [|"first", "second", "third"|];
let list = Array.to_list(array);
```

But we can also map over a list directly:

```
/* Belt standard library */
let list = ["first", "second", "third"];
Belt.List.map(list, e => e ++ "-mapped");

/* Reason standard library */
let list = ["first", "second", "third"];
List.map(e => e ++ "-mapped", list);
```

Logging `list` to the console shows that lists are represented as nested arrays in JavaScript where each array always has two elements:

```
["first", ["second", ["third", 0]]]
```

This makes sense after understanding that a list is a recursive data structure. Reason lists are **singly linked lists**. Each element in a list is either **empty** (represented as 0 in JavaScript) or the **combination** of a value and another list.

An example type definition for list reveals that list is a variant:

```
type list('a) = Empty | Head('a, list('a));
```

> **Note**: type definitions can be recursive.

Reason provides some syntactic sugar that simplifies its more verbose version:

```
Head("first", Head("second", Head("third", Empty)));
```

Recursion

Since list is a recursive data structure, we typically use recursion when working with it.

To get warmed up, let's write a (naive) function that sums a list of integers:

```
let rec sum = list => switch(list) {
  | [] => 0
  | [hd, ...tl] => hd + sum(tl)
};
```

- This is a recursive function and therefore requires the rec keyword (that is, let rec instead of just let)
- We can pattern match on a list (just like any other variant and many other data structures)
- From the example type definition, Empty is represented as [] and Head is represented as [hd, ...tl] where hd is the **head** of the list and tl is the rest (that is, the **tail**) of the list
- tl could be [] (that is, Empty) and when it is, recursion stops

Passing sum the list [1, 2, 3] results in the following steps:

```
sum([1, 2, 3])
1 + sum([2, 3])
1 + 2 + sum([3])
1 + 2 + 3
6
```

Let's get a bit more comfortable with lists and recursion by analyzing another (naive) function that reverses a list:

```
let rec reverse = list => switch(list) {
  | [] => []
  | [hd, ...tl] => reverse(tl) @ [hd]
};
```

- Again, we use `rec` to define a recursive function
- Again, we use pattern matching on the list—if it's empty, stop recursion; otherwise, continue with a smaller list
- The `@` operator appends the second list to the end of the first list

Passing in the previously defined list (`["first", "second", "third"]`) results in the following steps:

```
reverse(["first", "second", "third"])
reverse(["second", "third"]) @ ["first"]
reverse(["third"]) @ ["second"] @ ["first"]
reverse([]) @ ["third"] @ ["second"] @ ["first"]
[] @ ["third"] @ ["second"] @ ["first"]
["third", "second", "first"]
```

This implementation of reverse is naive for two reasons:

- It's not tail call optimized (nor is our `sum` function)
- It uses append (`@`), which is slower than `prepend`

A better implementation would be to use a local helper function with an accumulator:

```
let reverse = list => {
  let rec aux = (list, acc) => switch(list) {
    | [] => acc
    | [hd, ...tl] => aux(tl, [hd, ...acc])
  };
  aux(list, []);
};
```

Now, its tail call is optimized and it uses prepend instead of append. In Reason, you prepend to a list using the ... syntax:

```
let list = ["first", "second", "third"];
let list = ["prepended", ...list];
```

Passing in the list (`["first", "second", "third"]`) roughly results in the following steps:

```
reverse(["first", "second", "third"])
aux(["first", "second", "third"], [])
aux(["second", "third"], ["first"])
aux(["third"], ["second", "first"])
aux([], ["third", "second", "first"])
["third", "second", "first"]
```

Notice that in the non-tail recursive version, Reason cannot create the list until recursion completes. In the tail recursive version, the accumulator (that is, the second argument of `aux`) is updated after each iteration.

Tail recursive (that is, tail call optimized) functions have the benefit of being able to reuse the current stack frame. As a result, tail recursive functions will never have a stack overflow, but non-tail recursive functions may have a stack overflow given enough iterations.

Pipe operators

Reason has two pipe operators:

```
|>  (pipe)
->  (fast pipe)
```

Both pipe operators pass arguments to functions. The `|>` pipe operator pipes to a function's last argument and the `->` fast pipe operator pipes to a function's first argument.

Take a look at these:

```
three |> f(one, two)
one -> f(two, three)
```

They are equivalent to this:

```
f(one, two, three)
```

If the function only accepts one argument, then both pipes work the same, since the function's first argument is also the function's last argument.

Using these pipe operators is quite popular, since, once you get the hang of it, it makes the code a lot more readable.

We don't need to use this:

```
Belt.List.(reduce(map([1, 2, 3], e => e + 1), 0, (+)))
```

We can write it in a way that doesn't require the reader to read it inside out:

```
Belt.List.(
  [1, 2, 3]
  ->map(e => e + 1)
  ->reduce(0, (+))
);
```

As you can see, using fast pipe looks similar to chaining in JavaScript. Unlike JavaScript, we can pass reduce the + function, since it is just a normal function that accepts two arguments and adds them. The parentheses are necessary to tell Reason to treat the infix operator (+) as an identifier.

Using Belt

Let's use what we've learned so far in this chapter to write a small program that creates a deck of cards, shuffles it, and draws five cards from the top of the deck. To do so, we'll use Belt's `Option` and `List` modules, as well as the fast pipe operator.

Option module

Belt's `Option` module is a collection of utility functions for working with the `option` type. For example, to unwrap an option and throw a runtime exception if the option's value is `None`, we can use `getExn`:

```
let foo = Some(3)->Belt.Option.getExn;
Js.log(foo); /* 3 */

let foo = None->Belt.Option.getExn;
Js.log(foo); /* raises getExn exception */
```

> Belt functions that are able to throw runtime exceptions always have the `Exn` suffix.

An alternative function to unwrap an option that isn't able to throw a runtime exception is `getWithDefault`:

```
let foo = None->Belt.Option.getWithDefault(0);
Js.log(foo); /* 0 */
```

The `Option` module provides several other functions such as `isSome`, `isNone`, `map`, `mapWithDefault`, and more. Check the documentation for details.

> Belt Option module documentation can be found here:
>
> https://bucklescript.github.io/bucklescript/api/Belt.Option.html

List module

List module are the utilities for list data types. To see what functions Belt provides for working with lists, inspect Belt's `List` modules documentation.

> Belt List module documentation can be found here:
>
> https://bucklescript.github.io/bucklescript/api/Belt.List.html

Let's focus on a few of them.

make

The `make` function is used to create a populated list. It accepts an integer for the length of the list and a value for each item in the list. Its type is as follows:

```
(int, 'a) => Belt.List.t('a)
```

`Belt.List.t` is exposed as an alias of the `list` type, so we can say the type of `Belt.List.make` is as follows:

```
(int, 'a) => list('a)
```

We can use it to create a list containing ten strings, like so:

```
let list = Belt.List.make(10, "string");
```

In Chapter 5, *Effective ML*, we will learn about how to explicitly expose or hide types and bindings from a module.

makeBy

The `makeBy` function is like the `make` function, except it accepts a function used to determine the value of each item given the item's index.

The type of the `makeBy` function is as follows:

```
(int, int => 'a) => Belt.List.t('a)
```

We can use it to create a list of ten items, where each item is equal to its index:

```
let list = Belt.List.makeBy(10, i => i);
```

shuffle

The `shuffle` function randomly shuffles a list. It has type:

```
Belt.List.t('a) => Belt.List.t('a)
```

It accepts a list and returns a new list. Let's use it to shuffle our list of integers:

```
let list = Belt.List.(makeBy(10, i => i)->shuffle);
```

take

The `take` function accepts a list and a length and returns a subset of the list starting from the head of the list with length equal to the requested length. Since the requested length of the subset may exceed the original list's length, the result is wrapped in an option. Its type is as follows:

```
(Belt.List.t('a), int) => option(Belt.List.t('a))
```

We can take the first two items from our shuffled list, like so:

```
let list = Belt.List.(makeBy(10, i => i)->shuffle->take(2));
```

Deck of cards example

Now, we're ready to combine this with what we've learned from previous chapters. How would you write a program that creates a deck of cards, shuffles it, and draws the first five cards? Before looking at the following example, give it a shot yourself.

```
type suit =
  | Hearts
  | Diamonds
  | Spades
  | Clubs;

type card = {
  suit,
  rank: int,
};

Belt.List.(
  makeBy(52, i =>
    switch (i / 13, i mod 13) {
    | (0, rank) => {suit: Hearts, rank: rank + 1}
    | (1, rank) => {suit: Diamonds, rank: rank + 1}
    | (2, rank) => {suit: Spades, rank: rank + 1}
    | (3, rank) => {suit: Clubs, rank: rank + 1}
    | _ => assert(false)
    }
  )
  ->shuffle
  ->take(5)
  ->Belt.Option.getExn
  ->(
      cards => {
        let rankToString = rank =>
          switch (rank) {
          | 1 => "Ace"
          | 13 => "King"
          | 12 => "Queen"
          | 11 => "Jack"
          | rank => string_of_int(rank)
          };

        let suitToString = suit =>
          switch (suit) {
          | Hearts => "Hearts"
          | Diamonds => "Diamonds"
          | Spades => "Spades"
          | Clubs => "Clubs"
          };
```

```
          map(cards, ({rank, suit}) =>
            rankToString(rank) ++ " of " ++ suitToString(suit)
          );
      }
    )
  ->toArray
  ->Js.log
);
```

This yields an array of five cards at random in string format:

```
[
  "Queen of Clubs",
  "4 of Clubs",
  "King of Spades",
  "Ace of Hearts",
  "9 of Spades"
]
```

Currying

Some of the Belt standard library functions have a *U* suffix, such as this one:

```
Belt.List.makeBy
```

You can see the suffix here:

```
Belt.List.makeByU
```

The *U* suffix stands for *uncurried*. Before going further, let's define currying.

In Reason, every function accepts exactly one argument. This seems to contradict many of our earlier examples:

```
let add = (a, b) => a + b;
```

The preceding add function looks as if it accepts two arguments, but it is actually just syntactic sugar for the following:

```
let add = a => b => a + b;
```

The add function accepts a single argument, a, which returns a function that accepts a single argument, b, and then returns the result of a + b.

In Reason, both versions are valid and have the same compiled output. In JavaScript, both of the preceding versions are valid, but they are not the same; they would need to be used differently to get the same result. The second would need to be called like so:

```
add(2)(3);
```

This is because `add` returns a function that then needs to be called again, hence the two sets of parenthesis. Reason would accept either usage:

```
add(2, 3);
add(2)(3);
```

The benefit of currying is that it makes composing functions easier. You can easily create a function, `addOne`, that is partially applied:

```
let addOne = add(1);
```

This `addOne` function could then be passed to other functions such as `map`. Perhaps you'd like to use this feature to pass a function to a ReasonReact child component with the parent component's `self` partially applied.

Confusingly, the compiled output of either version of `add` is as follows:

```
function add(a, b) {
   return a + b | 0;
}
```

Where is the intermediate function? Wherever possible, BuckleScript optimizes the compiled output to avoid the unnecessary function allocation, which improves performance.

Remember, since Reason's infix operators are just normal functions, we could have just done the following:

```
let addOne = (+)(1);
```

Uncurried functions

Due to JavaScript's dynamic nature, BuckleScript cannot always optimize the compiled output to remove the intermediate functions. However, you can tell BuckleScript to uncurry a function using the following syntax:

```
let add = (. a, b) => a + b;
```

The uncurry syntax is the dot in the argument list. It needs to be present at both the declaration and call sites:

```
let result = add(. 2, 3); /* 5 */
```

BuckleScript will throw a compile time error if the call site isn't using the uncurry syntax:

```
let result = add(2, 3);

We've found a bug for you!

This is an uncurried BuckleScript function. It must be applied with a dot.

Like this: foo(. a, b)
Not like this: foo(a, b)
```

Also, a compile time error is thrown if some of the function's arguments are missing at the call site:

```
let result = add(. 2);

We've found a bug for you!

Found uncurried application [@bs] with arity 2, where arity 1 was expected.
```

The term `arity` refers to the number of arguments a function accepts.

makeByU

We can replace `makeBy` with `makeByU` if we uncurry its second argument. This will improve performance (a negligible amount in our example):

```
...
makeByU(52, (. i) =>
  switch (i / 13, i mod 13) {
  | (0, rank) => {suit: Hearts, rank: rank + 1}
  | (1, rank) => {suit: Diamonds, rank: rank + 1}
  | (2, rank) => {suit: Spades, rank: rank + 1}
  | (3, rank) => {suit: Clubs, rank: rank + 1}
  | _ => assert(false)
  }
)
...
```

The dot syntax requires parentheses around `i`.

JavaScript interoperability

The term **interoperability** refers to the ability for Reason programs to use existing JavaScript within Reason. BuckleScript provides an excellent system for using existing JavaScript code within Reason, and also makes it easy to use Reason code within JavaScript.

Using JavaScript in Reason

We've already seen how we can use raw JavaScript in Reason. Let's now focus on how to bind to existing JavaScript. To bind a value to a named reference, we typically use `let`. That binding can then be used in subsequent code. When the value we want to bind to lives is JavaScript, we use `external`. The `external` binding is like a `let`, in the sense that it can be used in subsequent code. Unlike `let`, `external` is typically accompanied by BuckleScript decorators such as `[@bs.val]`.

Understanding the [@bs.val] decorator

We can use `[@bs.val]` to bind to global values and functions. In general, the syntax is as follows:

```
[@bs.val] external alert: string => unit = "alert";
```

- One or more BuckleScript decorators (that is, `[@bs.val]`)
- The `external` keyword
- The binding's named reference
- The type declaration
- An equal sign
- A string

The external keyword binds `alert` to a value of type `string => unit` and is bound to the string `alert`. The string `alert` is the value of the above external declaration and is what is going to be used in the compiled output. When the name of the external binding is equal to its string value, the string can be left empty:

```
[@bs.val] external alert: string => unit = "";
```

Using the binding is just like using any other binding:

```
alert("hi!");
```

Understanding the [@bs.scope] decorator

To bind to `window.location.pathname`, we add a scope using `[@bs.scope]`. This defines the scope for `[@bs.val]`. For example, if you want to bind to the `pathname` property of `window.location`, you can specify the scope as `[@bs.scope ("window", "location")]`:

```
[@bs.val] [@bs.scope ("window", "location")] external pathname: string = "";
```

Or, we could include the scope in the string using only `[@bs.val]`:

```
[@bs.val] external pathname: string = "window.location.pathname";
```

Understanding the [@bs.send] decorator

The `[@bs.send]` decorator is for binding to an object's methods and properties. When using `[@bs.send]`, the first argument is always the object. If there are remaining arguments, they will get applied to the object's method:

```
[@bs.val] external document: Dom.document = "";
[@bs.send] external getElementById: (Dom.document, string) => Dom.element = "";
let element = getElementById(document, "root");
```

The `Dom` module is also provided by BuckleScript and provides type declarations for the DOM.

> The Dom module documentation can be found here:
>
> https://bucklescript.github.io/bucklescript/api/Dom.html
>
> There is also a Node module for use with Node.js:
>
> https://bucklescript.github.io/bucklescript/api/Node.html

Be careful when writing external declarations since you can accidentally lie to the type system, which could result in runtime type errors. For example, we told Reason that our `getElementById` binding always returns a `Dom.element`, but it returns `undefined` when the DOM can't find an element with the provided ID. A more correct binding would be this:

```
[@bs.send] external getElementById: (Dom.document, string) =>
option(Dom.element) = "";
```

Understanding the [@bs.module] decorator

To import a node module, use `[@bs.module]`. The compiled output depends on the `package-specs` configuration used within `bsconfig.json`. We're using es6 as the module format.

```
[@bs.module] external leftPad: (string, int) => string = "left-pad";
let result = leftPad("foo", 6);
```

This compiles to the following:

```
import * as LeftPad from "left-pad";

var result = LeftPad("foo", 6);

export {
  result ,
}
```

Setting the module format to `commonjs` results in the following compiled output:

```
var LeftPad = require("left-pad");

var result = LeftPad("foo", 6);

exports.result = result;
```

When there is no string argument to `[@bs.module]`, the default value is imported.

Reasonable APIs

When binding to existing JavaScript APIs, think about how you'd like to use the API in Reason. Even existing JavaScript APIs that rely heavily on JavaScript's dynamic typing can be used in Reason. BuckleScript leverages advanced type system techniques that let us take advantage of Reason's type system with such APIs.

From the BuckleScript documentation, take a look at the following JavaScript function:

```
function padLeft(value, padding) {
  if (typeof padding === "number") {
    return Array(padding + 1).join(" ") + value;
  }
  if (typeof padding === "string") {
    return padding + value;
  }
  throw new Error(`Expected string or number, got '${padding}'.`);
}
```

If we were to bind to this function in Reason, it would be nice to use `padding` as a variant. Here is how we would do that:

```
[@bs.val]
external padLeft: (
  string,
  [@bs.unwrap] [
    | `Str(string)
    | `Int(int)
  ])
  => string = "";

padLeft("Hello World", `Int(4));
padLeft("Hello World", `Str("Message: "));
```

This compiles to the following:

```
padLeft("Hello World", 4);
padLeft("Hello World", "Message: ");
```

The type of `padLeft` is `(string, some_variant) => string`, where `some_variant` uses an advanced type system feature called **polymorphic variant**, which that uses `[@bs.unwrap]` to get converted to something JavaScript can understand. We'll learn more about polymorphic variants in `Chapter 5`, *Effective ML*.

BuckleScript documentation

Although this was just a brief introduction, you can see that BuckleScript has a lot of tools to help us communicate with idiomatic JavaScript. I highly encourage you to read the BuckleScript docs to learn more about JavaScript interoperability.

BuckleScript, Belt, and Interoperability

> BuckleScript documentation can be found here:
>
> https://bucklescript.github.io/docs/interop-overview

Binding to existing ReactJS components

ReactJS components are not Reason components. To use an existing ReactJS component, we use [@bs.module] to import the node module, and then use the ReasonReact.wrapJsForReason helper function to convert the ReactJS component to a Reason component. There is also a ReasonReact.wrapReasonForJs helper function for using Reason in ReactJS.

Let's resume building our app from where we left off in Chapter 3, *Creating ReasonReact Components*:

```
git clone https://github.com/PacktPublishing/ReasonML-Quick-Start-Guide.git
cd ReasonML-Quick-Start-Guide
cd Chapter03/app-end
npm install
```

Here, we'll add route transitions by binding to the existing React Transition Group components:

> React Transition Group documentation can be found here:
>
> https://reactcommunity.org/react-transition-group/

Importing dependencies

Run npm install --save react-transition-group to install the dependency.

Let's create a new file called ReactTransitionGroup.re to house these bindings. In this file, we'll bind to the TransitionGroup and CSSTransition components:

```
[@bs.module "react-transition-group"]
external transitionGroup: ReasonReact.reactClass = "TransitionGroup";

[@bs.module "react-transition-group"]
external cssTransition: ReasonReact.reactClass = "CSSTransition";
```

Creating the make functions

Next, we create the components' required `make` functions. This is where we use the `ReasonReact.wrapJsForReason` helper function.

For `TransitionGroup`, we won't need any props. Since the `~props` argument is required, we pass `Js.Obj.empty()`. The `~reactClass` argument is passed the external binding we created in the previous step:

```
module TransitionGroup = {
  let make = children =>
    ReasonReact.wrapJsForReason(
      ~reactClass=transitionGroup,
      ~props=Js.Obj.empty(),
      children,
    );
};
```

Now, `ReactTransitionGroup.TransitionGroup` is a ReasonReact component that can be used in our app.

Using [@bs.deriving abstract]

`CSSTransitionGroup` will need the following props:

- `_in`
- `timeout`
- `classNames`

Since `in` is a reserved word in Reason, the convention is to use `_in` in Reason and have BuckleScript compile it to `in` for JavaScript using `[@bs.as "in"]`.

BuckleScript provides `[@bs.deriving abstract]` for easily working with certain types of JavaScript objects. Instead of creating an object in JavaScript and binding to that object, we can create that object directly using BuckleScript:

```
[@bs.deriving abstract]
type cssTransitionProps = {
  [@bs.as "in"] _in: bool,
  timeout: int,
  classNames: string,
};
```

BuckleScript, Belt, and Interoperability

> **Note:** `cssTransitionProps` is not a record type, it just looks like one.

When using `[@bs.deriving abstract]`, a helper function is automatically provided to create JavaScript objects of that shape. This helper function is also named `cssTransitionProps`. We use this helper function in the component's `make` function to create the component's props:

```
module CSSTransition = {
  let make = (~_in: bool, ~timeout: int, ~classNames: string, children) =>
    ReasonReact.wrapJsForReason(
      ~reactClass=cssTransition,
      ~props=cssTransitionProps(~_in, ~timeout, ~classNames),
      children,
    );
};
```

Using the components

Now, in `App.re`, we can change the render function to use these components. We'll change this:

```
<main> {currentRoute.component} </main>
```

Now it appears as follows:

```
<main>
  ReactTransitionGroup.(
    <TransitionGroup>
      <CSSTransition
         key={currentRoute.title} _in=true timeout=900 classNames="routeTransition">
        {currentRoute.component}
      </CSSTransition>
    </TransitionGroup>
  )
</main>
```

[98]

> Note: The key prop is a special ReactJS prop and should not be part of the component's props argument in `ReasonReact.wrapJsForReason`. The same is true for the special ReactJS ref prop.

For completeness, here is the corresponding CSS, which can be found in `ReactTransitionGroup.scss`:

```scss
@keyframes enter {
  from {
    opacity: 0;
    transform: translateY(50px);
  }
}

@keyframes exit {
  to {
    opacity: 0;
    transform: translateY(50px);
  }
}

.routeTransition-enter.routeTransition-enter-active {
  animation: enter 500ms ease 400ms both;
}

.routeTransition-exit.routeTransition-exit-active {
  animation: exit 400ms ease both;
}
```

Be sure to require the preceding in `ReactTransitionGroup.re`:

```
/* ReactTransitionGroup.re */
[@bs.val] external require: string => string = "";
require("../../../src/ReactTransitionGroup.scss");
```

Now, when changing routes, the old route's content animates down and fades out before the new route's content animates up and fades in.

Summary

BuckleScript is incredibly powerful because it lets us interoperate with idiomatic JavaScript in a very pleasant way. It also provides the Belt standard library, which was created with JavaScript in mind. We learned about arrays and lists, and we saw how easy it is to use existing ReactJS components within Reason.

In `Chapter 5`, *Effective ML*, we'll learn about how to use module signatures to hide a component's implementation details while building an autocomplete input component. We'll start with hardcoded data at first, and in `Chapter 6`, *CSS-in-JS (in Reason)*, we'll move that data to `localStorage` (client-side web storage).

5
Effective ML

So far, we've learned the basics of Reason. We've seen how having a sound type system can make refactoring a safer, less stressful endeavor. When changing an implementation detail, the type system helpfully alerts us to the other areas of the codebase that need to be updated. In this chapter, we'll learn how to hide implementation details to make refactoring even easier. By hiding implementation details, we guarantee that changing them won't affect other areas of your codebase.

We'll also learn how the type system can help us enforce business rules in our application. Hiding implementation details also gives us a nice way to enforce business rules by guaranteeing that modules are not being misused by the user. We'll illustrate this point throughout much of this chapter using simple code examples that are included in this book's GitHub repository.

To follow along, start from `Chapter05/app-start`. These examples are isolated from the app we've been building.

You can go to the GitHub repository for this book using the following:

```
git clone https://github.com/PacktPublishing/ReasonML-Quick-Start-Guide.git
cd ReasonML-Quick-Start-Guide
cd Chapter05/app-start
npm install
```

Remember, all modules are global and all of a module's types and bindings are exposed by default. As we'll soon see, module signatures can be used to hide a module's types and/or bindings from other modules. In this chapter, we'll also learn about advanced type system features, including the following:

- Abstract types
- Phantom types
- Polymorphic variants

Module signatures

A module signature constrains a module in a similar way to how an interface can constrain a class in object-oriented programming. A module signature can require that a module implements certain types and bindings and can also be used to hide implementation details. Say that we had a module called `Foo` defined in `Foo.re`. Its signature can be defined in `Foo.rei`. Any type or binding listed in a module's signature is exposed to other modules. Any type or binding listed in a module is hidden if a module signature exists and that type or binding isn't present in the module signature. Given a binding `let foo = "foo";` in `Foo.re`, that binding can be both required and exposed by its module signature by including `let foo: string;` in `Foo.rei`:

```
/* Foo.re */
let foo = "foo";

/* Foo.rei */
let foo: string;

/* Bar.re */
Js.log(Foo.foo);
```

Here, `Foo.rei` requires `Foo.re` to have a `let` binding named `foo` of the `string` type.

If a module's `.rei` file exists and is empty, then everything within the module is hidden, as shown in the following code:

```
/* Foo.rei */
/* this is intentionally empty */

/* Bar.re */
Js.log(Foo.foo); /* Compilation error: The value foo can't be found in Foo */
```

A module's signature requires the module to include any types and/or bindings listed in the signature, as shown in the following code:

```
/* Foo.re */
let foo = "foo";

/* Foo.rei */
let foo: string;
let bar: string;
```

This results in the following compilation error because the module signature requires a `bar` binding of the `string` type that isn't defined in the module:

```
The implementation src/Foo.re does not match the interface src/Foo.rei:
The value `bar' is required but not provided
```

Module types

A module signature can also be defined using the `module type` keyword instead of using a separate `.rei` file. The module type must start with a capital letter. Once defined, a module can be constrained by a module type using the `module <Name> : <Type>` syntax, as follows:

```
module type FooT {
  let foo: (~a: int, ~b: int) => int;
};

module Foo: FooT {
  let foo = (~a, ~b) => a + b;
};
```

The same module type can be used for multiple modules, as follows:

```
module Bar: FooT {
  let bar = (~a, ~b) => a - b;
};
```

We can think of module signatures as interfaces in the object-oriented sense. The interface defines the properties and methods that a module must define. In Reason, however, module signatures also hide bindings and types. But perhaps one of the most useful features of module signatures is the ability to expose abstract types.

Abstract types

Abstract types are type declarations that don't have a definition. Let's explore why this would be useful. In addition to bindings, module signatures can include types. In the following code, you'll notice that the module signature of `Foo` includes a `person` type, and now `Foo` must include this `type` declaration:

```
/* Foo.re */
type person = {
  firstName: string,
  lastName: string
```

[103]

Effective ML

```
};

/* Foo.rei */
type person = {
  firstName: string,
  lastName: string
};
```

The `person` type is exposed in the same way as if there were no module signature defined. As you'd expect, if a signature is defined and the type is not listed, the type isn't exposed to other modules. There is also the option to leave the type abstract. We only keep what's left of the equals sign. Let's look at the following code:

```
/* Foo.rei */
type person;
```

Now, the `person` type is exposed to other modules, but no other modules can directly create or manipulate a value of the `person` type. The `person` type is required to be defined in `Foo`, but it can have any definition. This means that the `person` type can change over time, and no modules outside of `Foo` would ever know the difference.

Let's explore abstract types further in the following section.

Using module signatures

Let's imagine that we're building an invoice-management system and we have an `Invoice` module that defines an `invoice` type along with a function that other modules can use to create values of that type. This arrangement is shown in the following code:

```
/* Invoice.re */
type t = {
  name: string,
  email: string,
  date: Js.Date.t,
  total: float
};

let make = (~name, ~email, ~date, ~total) => {
  name,
  email,
  date,
  total
};
```

Let's also suppose that we have another module that is responsible for sending emails to customers, as shown in the following code:

```
/* Email.re */
let send = invoice: Invoice.t => ...
let invoice =
  Invoice.make(
    ~name="Raphael",
    ~email="persianturtle@gmail.com",
    ~date=Js.Date.make(),
    ~total=15.0,
  );
send(invoice);
```

Since the `Invoice.t` type is exposed, the invoice can be manipulated by `Email`, as shown in the following code:

```
/* Email.re */
let invoice =
  Invoice.make(
    ~name="Raphael",
    ~email="persianturtle@gmail.com",
    ~date=Js.Date.make(),
    ~total=15.0,
  );
let invoice = {...invoice, total: invoice.total *. 0.8};
Js.log(invoice);
```

Despite the `Invoice.t` type being immutable, there is nothing preventing `Email` from shadowing the invoice binding with some altered fields. However, if we made the `Invoice.t` type abstract, this wouldn't be possible because `Email` wouldn't be able to manipulate the abstract type. None of the functions that the `Email` module has access to would work with an `Invoice.t` type.

```
/* Invoice.rei */
type t;
let make:
  (~name: string, ~email: string, ~date: Js.Date.t, ~total: float) => t;
```

Now, compiling gives us the following error:

```
8 | let invoice = {...invoice, total: invoice.total *. 0.8};
9 | Js.log(invoice);

The record field total can't be found.
```

Effective ML

If we decide to allow other modules to add discounts to invoices, we would need to create a function and include it in the module signature of Invoice. Let's suppose we want to only allow one discount per invoice and also restrict the discount amount to ten, fifteen, or twenty percent. We could implement this in the following way:

```
/* Invoice.re */
type t = {
 name: string,
 email: string,
 date: Js.Date.t,
 total: float,
 isDiscounted: bool,
};

type discount =
 | Ten
 | Fifteen
 | Twenty;

let make = (~name, ~email, ~date, ~total) => {
 name,
 email,
 date,
 total,
 isDiscounted: false,
};

let discount = (~invoice, ~discount) =>
 if (invoice.isDiscounted) {
 invoice;
 } else {
 {
 ...invoice,
 isDiscounted: true,
 total:
 invoice.total
 *. (
 switch (discount) {
 | Ten => 0.9
 | Fifteen => 0.85
 | Twenty => 0.8
 }
 ),
 };
 };

/* Invoice.rei */
```

[106]

```
type t;

type discount =
  | Ten
  | Fifteen
  | Twenty;

let make:
  (~name: string, ~email: string, ~date: Js.Date.t, ~total: float) => t;

let discount: (~invoice: t, ~discount: discount) => t;

/* Email.re */
let invoice =
 Invoice.make(
 ~name="Raphael",
 ~email="persianturtle@gmail.com",
 ~date=Js.Date.make(),
 ~total=15.0,
 );
Js.log(invoice);
```

Now, as long as the `Invoice` module's public API (or module signature) doesn't change, we're free to refactor the `Invoice` module however we'd like without needing to worry about breaking code in other modules. To prove this point, let's refactor `Invoice.t` to be a tuple instead of a record, as shown in the following code. As long as we don't change the module signature, the `Email` module won't need to change at all:

```
/* Invoice.re */
type t = (string, string, Js.Date.t, float, bool);

type discount =
  | Ten
  | Fifteen
  | Twenty;

let make = (~name, ~email, ~date, ~total) => (
  name,
  email,
  date,
  total,
  false,
);

let discount = (~invoice, ~discount) => {
  let (name, email, date, total, isDiscounted) = invoice;
  if (isDiscounted) {
```

```
      invoice;
    } else {
      (
        name,
        email,
        date,
        total
        *. (
          switch (discount) {
          | Ten => 0.9
          | Fifteen => 0.85
          | Twenty => 0.8
          }
        ),
        true,
      );
    };
};

/* Invoice.rei */
type t;

type discount =
  | Ten
  | Fifteen
  | Twenty;

let make:
  (~name: string, ~email: string, ~date: Js.Date.t, ~total: float) => t;

let discount: (~invoice: t, ~discount: discount) => t;

/* Email.re */
let invoice =
  Invoice.make(
    ~name="Raphael",
    ~email="persianturtle@gmail.com",
    ~date=Js.Date.make(),
    ~total=15.0,
  );
let invoice = Invoice.(discount(~invoice, ~discount=Ten));
Js.log(invoice);
```

Also, thanks to the `Invoice.t` abstract type, we are guaranteed that an invoice can only be discounted once, and only by specified percentages. We could take this example further by requiring all changes to an invoice to be logged. Traditionally, this sort of requirement would be solved by adding a side effect after a database transaction because, in JavaScript, we wouldn't otherwise be sure that we would be logging all changes to an invoice. With module signatures, we have the option to solve these kinds of requirements in the application layer.

Phantom types

Looking at our previous implementation, it would be nice if we didn't have to check whether an invoice has been discounted at runtime. Is there a way we could check whether an invoice has been discounted at compile time instead? With phantom types, we can.

Phantom types are types that have a type variable, but this type variable isn't used in its definition. To better understand, let's look again at the `option` type, as shown in the following code:

```
type option('a) =
  | None
  | Some('a);
```

The `option` type has a type variable, `'a`, and the type variable is being used in its definition. As we've already learned, `option` is a polymorphic type because it has a type variable. On the other hand, a phantom type doesn't use the type variable in its definition. Let's see how this is useful with our invoice management example.

Let's change the `Invoice` module's signature to use a phantom type, as follows:

```
/* Invoice.rei */
type t('a);

type discounted;
type undiscounted;

type discount =
  | Ten
  | Fifteen
  | Twenty;

let make:
  (~name: string, ~email: string, ~date: Js.Date.t, ~total: float) =>
  t(undiscounted);
```

Effective ML

```
let discount:
  (~invoice: t(undiscounted), ~discount: discount) => t(discounted);
```

The abstract `type t` is now `type t('a)`. We also have two more abstract types, as shown in the following code:

```
type discounted;
type undiscounted;
```

Also, note that the `make` function now returns `t(undiscounted)` (instead of just `t`) and the `discount` function now accepts `t(undiscounted)` and returns `t(discounted)`. Remember that the abstract `t('a)` accepts a `type` variable, and that the `type` variable just so happens to be either the `discounted` type or the `undiscounted` type.

In the implementation, we can now get rid of the runtime check we had previously, as shown in the following code:

```
if (isDiscounted) {
  ...
} else {
  ...
}
```

Now, this check is done at compile time since the `discount` function only accepts `undiscounted` invoices, as shown in the following code:

```
/* Invoice.re */
type t('a) = {
  name: string,
  email: string,
  date: Js.Date.t,
  total: float,
};

type discount =
  | Ten
  | Fifteen
  | Twenty;

let make = (~name, ~email, ~date, ~total) => {name, email, date, total};

let discount = (~invoice, ~discount) => {
  ...invoice,
  total:
    invoice.total
    *. (
      switch (discount) {
```

[110]

```
              | Ten => 0.9
              | Fifteen => 0.85
              | Twenty => 0.8
              }
        ),
  };
```

This is just one more way that a type system can help us focus more on logic and less on error handling. Previously, trying to discount an invoice twice would just return the original invoice unchanged. Let's now try to discount an invoice twice in `Email.re` using the following code:

```
/* Email.re */
let invoice =
  Invoice.make(
    ~name="Raphael",
    ~email="persianturtle@gmail.com",
    ~date=Js.Date.make(),
    ~total=15.0,
  );
let invoice = Invoice.(discount(~invoice, ~discount=Ten));
let invoice = Invoice.(discount(~invoice, ~discount=Ten)); /* discounted
twice */
Js.log(invoice);
```

Now, trying to discount an invoice twice will result in a lovely compile-time error, as follows:

```
We've found a bug for you!
   7 |  );
   8 |  let invoice = Invoice.(discount(~invoice, ~discount=Ten));
   9 |  let invoice = Invoice.(discount(~invoice, ~discount=Ten));
  10 |  Js.log(invoice);
This has type:
    Invoice.t(Invoice.discounted)
But somewhere wanted:
    Invoice.t(Invoice.undiscounted)
```

This is absolutely beautiful. Suppose, however, that you'd like to be able to email any invoice—discounted or not. Does our use of phantom types cause a problem? How would we write a function that takes any invoice type? We'll, remember that our invoice type is `Invoice.t('a)` and if we want to accept any invoice, we keep the type parameter, as shown in the following code:

```
/* Email.re */
let invoice =
  Invoice.make(
```

```
            ~name="Raphael",
            ~email="persianturtle@gmail.com",
            ~date=Js.Date.make(),
            ~total=15.0,
          );

          let send: Invoice.t('a) => unit = invoice => {
            /* send invoice email */
            Js.log(invoice);
          };

          send(invoice);
```

So we can have our cake and eat it too.

Polymorphic variants

We've already briefly looked at polymorphic variants in the previous chapter. To recap, we learned about them when we used the `[@bs.unwrap]` decorator to bind to some existing JavaScript. The idea was that `[@bs.unwrap]` can be used to bind to an existing JavaScript function where its arguments can be of different types. For example, let's say we want to bind to the following function:

```
function dynamic(a) {
  switch (typeof a) {
    case "string":
      return "String: " + a;
    case "number":
      return "Number: " + a;
  }
}
```

Let's say this function should only accept arguments of the `string` type or `int` type and nothing else. We could bind to this example function as follows:

```
[@bs.val] external dynamic : 'a => string = "";
```

However, our binding would then allow invalid argument types (such as `bool`). It would be better if our compiler could help us out by preventing invalid argument types. One way to do this is to use `[@bs.unwrap]` with a polymorphic variant. Our binding would then appear as follows:

```
[@bs.val] external dynamic : ([@bs.unwrap] [
  | `Str(string)
  | `Int(int)
]) => string = "";
```

We'd use the binding like so:

```
dynamic(`Int(42));
dynamic(`Str("foo"));
```

Now, if we tried to pass an invalid argument type, the compiler would let us know, as shown in the following code:

```
dynamic(42);

/*
We've found a bug for you!

This has type:
  int
But somewhere wanted:
  [ `Int of int | `Str of string ]
*/
```

The trade-off here is that we'll need to pass in arguments by wrapping them in the polymorphic variant constructors rather than directly.

Right off the bat, you'll notice the following two differences between normal variants and polymorphic variants:

1. We did not need to explicitly declare a type for the polymorphic variant
2. Polymorphic variants begin with a backtick character (`` ` ``)

Whenever you see a constructor prefixed with a backtick character, you know it's a polymorphic variant constructor. There may or may not be a type declaration associated with a polymorphic variant constructor.

Would this work with normal variants?

Let's try to do this with normal variants and see what happens:

```
type validArgs =
  | Int(int)
  | Str(string);

[@bs.val] external dynamic : validArgs => string = "";

dynamic(Int(1));
```

The problem with the preceding implementation is that `Int(1)` does not compile to a JavaScript number. Normal variants are compiled to an `array` and our `dynamic` function returns `undefined` instead of `"Number: 42"`. The function returns `undefined` because no cases on the switch statement were matched.

With polymorphic variants, BuckleScript compiles ``dynamic(`Int(42))`` to `dynamic(42)` and the function works as expected.

Advanced type system features

Reason's type system is quite full-featured and has been refined over the last couple of decades. What we've seen so far is only an introduction to Reason's type system. In my opinion, you should become familiar with the basics before continuing to more advanced type system features. It's hard to appreciate things such as type safety without having experienced bugs that a sound type system would have prevented. It's hard to appreciate advanced type system features without getting slightly frustrated with what you've learned so far in this book. It's beyond the scope of this book to discuss advanced type system features in too much detail, but I want to make sure that those of you who are evaluating Reason as an option know that there's much more to its type system.

In addition to phantom types and polymorphic variants, Reason has **generalized algebraic datatypes** (**GADTs**). Modules can be dynamically created using functors (that is, module functions that operate somewhere in between compile time and runtime). Reason also has classes and objects—the O in OCaml stands for objective. OCaml's predecessor was a language called Caml that first appeared in the mid 1980s. What we've learned so far in this book is specifically useful in the context of typical React applications. Personally, I like that Reason is a language that I can grow into while being productive.

If you find yourself frustrated with the type system, then reach out to the experts on the Discord channel and someone will likely help you work through your problem. I'm constantly amazed at how helpful the community is. And don't forget, if you just want to move on, you can always drop into raw JavaScript if you need to and come back to the problem when you're ready.

> You can find the Reason Discord channel here:
>
> `https://discord.gg/reasonml`

It's also perfectly valid to not use the fancier features of Reason's type system. What we've learned so far provides a lot of value in terms of adding type safety to our React applications.

Summary

By now, we've seen how Reason can help us build safer, more maintainable codebases with the help of its type system. Variants allow us make invalid states unrepresentable. The type system helps make refactoring a less scary, less painful process. Module signatures can help us to enforce business rules in our application. Module signatures also serve as basic documentation that lists what a module exposes and gives you a basic idea of how the module is meant to be used based on exposed function names and their argument types, as well as exposed types.

In `Chapter 6`, *CSS-in-JS (in Reason)*, we'll look at how we can use Reason's type system to enforce valid CSS using a CSS-in-Reason library that wraps Emotion (`https://emotion.sh`), called `bs-css`.

6
CSS-in-JS (in Reason)

One of the great things about React is that it lets us collocate a component's markup, behavior and styles in a single file. This collocation has cascading effects (no pun intended) on the developer experience, version control, and code quality over time. In this chapter, we'll briefly explore what CSS-in-JS is and how we can approach CSS-in-JS in Reason. Of course, it's perfectly valid to break a component up across separate files and/or use a more traditional CSS solution, if that's what you prefer.

In this chapter, we will be looking at the following topics:

- What is CSS-in-JS?
- Using `styled-components`
- Using `bs-css`

What is CSS-in-JS?

Defining CSS-in-JS is currently a polarizing topic in the JavaScript community. CSS-in-JS was born during the component age. The modern web is largely built with the component model. Pretty much all JavaScript frameworks have embraced it. As its adoption grew, more and more teams started working on various components of the same project. Imagine that you're working on a large app in a distributed team and each team is working on a component in parallel. Without having the team standardize CSS conventions, you're going to run into CSS scoping issues. Without some type of standardized CSS style guide, it's going to be easy for multiple teams to style a class name such that other unintended components are affected. Over time, a number of solutions emerged to solve this and other related problems with CSS at-scale.

A brief history

Some CSS conventions that became popular include BEM, SMACSS, and OOCSS. Each of these solutions required developers to learn the convention and remember to apply it correctly; otherwise, frustrating scoping issues could still occur.

CSS modules became a safer option, where developers would import CSS into JavaScript modules and a build step would automatically scope that CSS locally to that JavaScript module. The CSS itself is still written in a normal CSS (or SASS) file.

CSS-in-JS went one step further and allowed you to write your CSS directly in your JavaScript module, automatically scoping that CSS locally to the component. This felt right for a lot of developers; others didn't like it from the start. Some CSS-in-JS solutions, such as styled-components, allow developers to couple CSS together with components directly. Instead of <header className="..." />, you could have <Header />, where the Header component is defined using styled-components and its CSS, as shown in the following code:

```
import React from 'react';
import styled from 'styled-components';

const Header = styled.header`
  font-size: 1.5em;
  text-align: center;
  color: dodgerblue;
`;
```

There was a time when styled-components had performance issues, since the JavaScript bundle had to download, compile, and execute before the library could create style sheets dynamically in the DOM. These problems have now been largely solved thanks to server-side rendering support. So, are we able to do this in Reason? Let's see!

Using styled-components

One of the most loved features of styled-components is the ability to dynamically create CSS based on a component's props. One reason to use this feature is to create alternate versions of a component. These alternate versions would then be encapsulated within the styled component itself. The following is an example of a <Title /> where the text could be either centered or left-aligned and optionally underlined.

```
const Title = styled.h1`
  text-align: ${props => props.center ? "center" : "left"};
  text-decoration: ${props => props.underline ? "underline" : "none"};
```

```
    color: white;
    background-color: coral;
`;

render(
  <div>
    <Title>I'm Left Aligned</Title>
    <Title center>I'm Centered!</Title>
    <Title center underline>I'm Centered & Underlined!</Title>
  </div>
);
```

The challenge in the context of Reason lies in creating a component via the `styled-components` API that can work with props dynamically. Consider the following binding for the `styled.h1` function and our `<Title />` component.

```
/* StyledComponents.re */
[@bs.module "styled-components"] [@bs.scope "default"] [@bs.variadic]
external h1: (array(string), array('a)) => ReasonReact.reactClass = "h1";

module Title = {
  let title =
    h1(
      [|
        "text-align: ",
        "; text-decoration: ",
        "; color: white; background-color: coral;",
      |],
      [|
        props => props##center ? "center" : "left",
        props => props##underline ? "underline" : "none",
      |],
    );

  [@bs.deriving abstract]
  type jsProps = {
    center: bool,
    underline: bool,
  };

  let make = (~center=false, ~underline=false, children) =>
    ReasonReact.wrapJsForReason(
      ~reactClass=title,
      ~props=jsProps(~center, ~underline),
      children,
    );
};
```

CSS-in-JS (in Reason)

The `h1` function accepts an array of strings as its first argument, and an array of expressions as its second argument. This is because that is the ES5 representation of ES6-tagged template literals. In the case of the `h1` function, the array of expressions are functions of the props passed to the React component.

We're using the `[@bs.variadic]` decorator to allow an arbitrary number of arguments. On the Reason side, we use an array, and on the JavaScript side the array is expanded as an arbitrary number of arguments.

Using [@bs.variadic]

Let's go off on a quick tangent to explore `[@bs.variadic]` a bit further. Let's assume you'd like to bind to `Math.max()`, which can take one or more arguments:

```
/* JavaScript */
Math.max(1, 2);
Math.max(1, 2, 3, 4);
```

This is a perfect case for `[@bs.variadic]`. We use an array on the Reason side to hold the arguments, and the array will be expanded to match the above syntax in JavaScript.

```
/* Reason */
[@bs.scope "Math"][@bs.val][@bs.variadic] external max: array('a) => unit =
"";
max([|1, 2|]);
max([|1, 2, 3, 4|]);
```

Okay, we're back to the `styled-components` example. We can use the `<Title />` component as follows:

```
/* Home.re */
let component = ReasonReact.statelessComponent("Home");

let make = _children => {
  ...component,
  render: _self =>
    <StyledComponents.Title center=true underline=true>
      {ReasonReact.string("Page1")}
    </StyledComponents.Title>,
};
```

The preceding code is a styled ReasonReact component that renders an `h1` with some CSS. The CSS was defined previously within the `StyledComponents.Title` module. The `<Title />` component has two props—center and underline—both of which default to false.

Of course, this wouldn't be an elegant way to write styled components but it's functionally similar to the JavaScript version. Another option is to drop back into raw JavaScript to take advantage of the familiar tagged template literal syntax. Let's illustrate this example in `Title.re`.

```
/* Title.re */
%bs.raw
{|const styled = require("styled-components").default|};

let title = [%bs.raw
  {|
    styled.h1`
      text-align: ${props => props.center ? "center" : "left"};
      text-decoration: ${props => props.underline ? "underline" : "none"};
      color: white;
      background-color: coral;
    `
  |}
];

[@bs.deriving abstract]
type jsProps = {
  center: bool,
  underline: bool,
};

let make = (~center=false, ~underline=false, children) =>
  ReasonReact.wrapJsForReason(
    ~reactClass=title,
    ~props=jsProps(~center, ~underline),
    children,
  );
```

The usage would be similar, except that now the `<Title />` component is no longer a submodule of `StyledComponents`.

```
/* Home.re */
let component = ReasonReact.statelessComponent("Home");

let make = _children => {
  ...component,
  render: _self =>
```

```
    <Title center=true underline=true> {ReasonReact.string("Page1")}
</Title>,
};
```

Personally, I like the developer experience when using the [%bs.raw] version. I'd like to give Adam Coll (@acoll1) a big round of applause for coming up with both versions of the styled-components bindings. I'm also very excited to see what the community comes up with.

Let's now explore the community's most popular CSS-in-JS solution: bs-css.

Using bs-css

While there is no official recommendation from the Reason team for a CSS-in-JS solution, many are currently using a library called bs-css that wraps the emotion CSS-in-JS library (version 9). The bs-css library provides a type-safe API for use in Reason. With this approach, we can have the compiler check our CSS as well. We'll get a feel for this library by converting our App.scss, which we created in Chapter 3, *Creating ReasonReact Components*.

To follow along, clone this book's GitHub repository and start from Chapter06/app-start using the following code:

```
git clone https://github.com/PacktPublishing/ReasonML-Quick-Start-Guide.git
cd ReasonML-Quick-Start-Guide
cd Chapter06/app-start
npm install
```

To get started with bs-css, we'll include it as a dependency for both package.json and bsconfig.json as follows:

```
/* bsconfig.json */
...
"bs-dependencies": ["reason-react", "bs-css"],
...
```

After installing `bs-css` via npm and configuring `bsconfig.json`, we'll have access to the `Css` module provided by the library. It's standard practice to define your own submodule called `Styles`, where we open the `Css` module and write all of our CSS-in-Reason there. Since we'll be converting `App.scss`, we'll declare a `Styles` submodule in `App.re`, as follows:

```
/* App.re */

...
let component = ReasonReact.reducerComponent("App");

module Styles = {
  open Css;
};
...
```

Now, let's convert the following Sass:

```
.App {
  min-height: 100vh;

  &:after {
    content: "";
    transition: opacity 450ms cubic-bezier(0.23, 1, 0.32, 1),
      transform 0ms cubic-bezier(0.23, 1, 0.32, 1) 450ms;
    position: fixed;
    top: 0;
    right: 0;
    bottom: 0;
    left: 0;
    background-color: rgba(0, 0, 0, 0.33);
    transform: translateX(-100%);
    opacity: 0;
    z-index: 1;
  }

  &.overlay {
    &:after {
      transition: opacity 450ms cubic-bezier(0.23, 1, 0.32, 1);
      transform: translateX(0%);
      opacity: 1;
    }
  }
}
```

Inside `Styles`, we declare a binding called `app` that will be used later in the `<App />` component's `className` prop. We'll bind to the result of a `bs-css` function called `style`. The `style` function takes in a list of CSS rules. Let's explore the syntax using the following code:

```
module Styles = {
  open Css;

  let app = style([
    minHeight(vh(100.)),
  ]);
};
```

It's a bit weird at first, but the more you use it, the nicer it feels. All CSS properties and all units are functions. The functions have types. If the types don't match, the compiler will complain. Consider the following invalid CSS:

```
min-height: red;
```

This just silently fails in CSS, Sass, and even `styled-components`. With `bs-css`, we can at least prevent a lot of invalid CSS. The compiler will also inform us of any unused bindings, which can help us maintain CSS style sheets, and, as usual, we have full IntelliSense, which helps us learn the API as we go.

Personally, I'm a big fan of nesting CSS via Sass, and I'm thrilled that we can do the same with `bs-css`. To nest the `:after` pseudo selector, we use the `after` function. To nest the `.overlay` selector, we use the `selector` function. Just like in Sass, we use the `&` symbol to reference the parent element, as shown in the following code:

```
module Styles = {
  open Css;

  let app =
    style([
      minHeight(vh(100.)),

      after([
contentRule(""),
transitions([
`transition("opacity 450ms cubic-bezier(0.23, 1, 0.32, 1)"),
`transition("transform 0ms cubic-bezier(0.23, 1, 0.32, 1) 450ms"),
]),
        position(fixed),
        top(zero),
        right(zero),
        bottom(zero),
```

[124]

```
            left(zero),
            backgroundColor(rgba(0, 0, 0, 0.33)),
            transform(translateX(pct(-100.))),
            opacity(0.),
            zIndex(1),
          ]),

          selector(
            "&.overlay",
            [
              after([
                `transition("opacity 450ms cubic-bezier(0.23, 1, 0.32, 1)"),
                transform(translateX(zero))),
                opacity(1.),
              ]),
            ],
          )
        ]);
    };
```

> Note how we are using the polymorphic variant `transition for the transition strings. Transitions are not valid otherwise.

You can find the rest of the conversion in the GitHub repository's Chapter06/app-end/src/App.re file. Now all that's left to do is apply the styles to the <App /> component's className prop, as shown in the following code:

```
/* App.re */
...
render: self =>
  <div
    className={"App " ++ Styles.app ++ (self.state.isOpen ? " overlay" : "")}
...
```

After deleting App.scss, everything looks mostly the same. Awesome! The exception is the nav > ul > li:after selector. In previous chapters, we used the content property to render an image, like so:

```
content: url(./img/icon/chevron.svg);
```

According to Css.rei, the contentRule function accepts a string. Therefore, using the url function does not typecheck, as shown in the following code:

```
contentRule(url("./img/icon/chevron.svg"))  /* type error */
```

CSS-in-JS (in Reason)

As an escape route, `bs-css` provides the `unsafe` function (as shown in the following code), which will bypass this problem:

```
unsafe("content", "url('./img/icon/chevron.svg')")
```

However, while our webpack configuration previously pulled the preceding image in as a dependency, it no longer does this when using `bs-css`.

Trade-offs

Using CSS-in-JS in Reason clearly is a trade-off. On the one hand, we can get type-safe, locally scoped CSS and we get to collocate our CSS with our components. On the other hand, the syntax is a bit more verbose and there may be some weird edge cases. It's perfectly valid to choose Sass over a CSS-in-JS solution as there is no clear winner here.

Other libraries

I encourage you to try other CSS-in-JS Reason libraries. And whenever you're looking for a Reason library, your first stop should be Redex (**Re**ason Package In**dex**).

> You can find Redex (**Re**ason Package In**dex**) at:
>
> `https://redex.github.io/`

Another helpful resource is the Reason Discord channel. It's a good place to ask about the various CSS-in-JS solutions and their trade-offs.

> You can find the Reason Discord channel at:
>
> `https://discord.gg/reasonml`

Summary

CSS-in-JS is still fairly new, and there will be a lot of experimentation with it in the Reason community in the near future. In this chapter, we learned about some of the benefits and challenges of CSS-in-JS (in Reason). Where do you stand?

In `Chapter 7`, *JSON in Reason*, we're going to learn about handling JSON in Reason and see how GraphQL can help reduce boilerplate code while achieving some pretty compelling guarantees.

7
JSON in Reason

In this chapter, we'll learn how to work with JSON by building a simple customer management application. This application lives within the `/customers` route of our existing app and can create, read, and update customers. JSON data persists to `localStorage`. Throughout this chapter, we convert external JSON into a typed data structure that Reason can understand in two different ways:

- Using pure Reason
- Using the `bs-json` library

We'll compare and contrast each method at the end of the chapter. We'll also discuss how **GraphQL** can help provide a pleasant developer experience when working with JSON in a statically typed language such as Reason.

To follow along with building the customer management application, clone this book's GitHub repository and start from `Chapter07/app-start`:

```
git clone https://github.com/PacktPublishing/ReasonML-Quick-Start-Guide.git
cd ReasonML-Quick-Start-Guide
cd Chapter07/app-start
npm install
```

In this chapter we will look at the following topics:

- Building views
- Integrating with localStorage
- Using bs-json
- Using GraphQL

Building views

In total, we'll have three views:

- A list view
- A create view
- An update view

Each view has its own route. The create and update views share a common component because they're so similar.

File structure

Since our `bsconfig.json` includes subdirectories, we can create a `src/customers` directory to house related components, and BuckleScript will recursively look for Reason (and OCaml) files in subdirectories of `src`:

```
/* bsconfig.json */
...
"sources": {
  "dir": "src",
  "subdirs": true
},
...
```

Let's move on and rename the `src/Page1.re` component to `src/customers/CustomerList.re`. In the same directory, we'll later create `Customer.re`, which will be used to both create and update individual customers.

Updating the router and navigation menu

In `Router.re`, we'll replace the `/page1` route with the following:

```
/* Router.re */
let routes = [
  ...
  {href: "/customers", title: "Customer List", component: <CustomerList />}
  ...
];
```

We'll also add the routes for /customers/create and /customers/:id:

```
/* Router.re */
let routes = [
  ...
  {href: "/customers/create", title: "Create Customer", component:
<Customer />,},
  {href: "/customers/:id", title: "Update Customer", component: <Customer
/>}
  ...
];
```

> The router has been updated so it can handle route variables (such as /customers/:id). This change has been made for you in Chapter07/app-start.

Finally, be sure to also update the navigation menu in <App.re />:

```
/* App.re */
render: self =>
  ...
  <ul>
    <li>
      <NavLink href="/customers">
        {ReasonReact.string("Customers")}
      </NavLink>
    </li>
    ...
```

CustomerType.re

This file will hold the customer type used by both <CustomerList /> and <Customer />. This is done to avoid any circular dependency compiler errors:

```
/* CustomerType.re */
type address = {
  street: string,
  city: string,
  state: string,
  zip: string,
};

type t = {
  id: int,
  name: string,
```

JSON in Reason

```
    address,
    phone: string,
    email: string,
};
```

CustomerList.re

For now, we'll use a hardcoded array of customers. Soon, we'll retrieve this data from `localStorage`. The following component renders a styled array of customers. Each customer is wrapped in a `<Link />` component. Clicking on a customer navigates to the update view:

```
let component = ReasonReact.statelessComponent("CustomerList");

let customers: array(CustomerType.t) = [
  {
    id: 1,
    name: "Christina Langworth",
    address: {
      street: "81 Casey Stravenue",
      city: "Beattyview",
      state: "TX",
      zip: "57918",
    },
    phone: "877-549-1362",
    email: "Christina.Langworth@gmail.com",
  },
  ...
];

module Styles = {
  open Css;

  let list =
    style([
      ...
    ]);
};

let make = _children => {
  ...component,
  render: _self =>
    <div>
      <ul className=Styles.list>
        {
          ReasonReact.array(
```

```
            Belt.Array.map(customers, customer =>
              <li key={string_of_int(customer.id)}>
                <Link href={"/customers/" ++ string_of_int(customer.id)}>
                  <p> {ReasonReact.string(customer.name)} </p>
                  <p> {ReasonReact.string(customer.address.street)} </p>
                  <p> {ReasonReact.string(customer.phone)} </p>
                  <p> {ReasonReact.string(customer.email)} </p>
                </Link>
              </li>
            )
          )
        }
      </ul>
    </div>,
};
```

Customer.re

This reducer component renders a form where every customer field is editable inside an input element. The component has two modes—`Create` and `Update`—based on the `window.location.pathname`.

We start by binding to `window.location.pathname`, and defining our component's actions and state:

```
/* Customer.re */
[@bs.val] external pathname: string = "window.location.pathname";

type mode =
  | Create
  | Update;

type state = {
  mode,
  customer: CustomerType.t,
};

type action =
  | Save(ReactEvent.Form.t);

let component = ReasonReact.reducerComponent("Customer");
```

JSON in Reason

Next, we add our component styles using `bs-css`. To see the styles, check out `Chapter07/app-end/src/customers/Customer.re`:

```
/* Customer.re */
module Styles = {
  open Css;

  let form =
    style([
      ...
    ]);
};
```

For now, we will use a hardcoded customer array, which we create in the following snippet. The full array can be found at `Chapter07/app-end/src/customers/Customer.re`:

```
/* Customer.re */
let customers: array(CustomerType.t) = [|
  {
    id: 1,
    name: "Christina Langworth",
    address: {
      street: "81 Casey Stravenue",
      city: "Beattyview",
      state: "TX",
      zip: "57918",
    },
    phone: "877-549-1362",
    email: "Christina.Langworth@gmail.com",
  },
  ...
|];
```

We also have helper functions, for the following reasons:

- To extract the customer ID from `window.location.pathname`
- To get a customer by ID
- To generate a default customer:

```
let getId = pathname =>
  try (Js.String.replaceByRe([%bs.re "/\\D/g"], "",
pathname)->int_of_string) {
  | _ => (-1)
  };

let getCustomer = customers => {
```

[134]

```
  let id = getId(pathname);
  customers |> Js.Array.find(customer => customer.CustomerType.id == id);
};

let getDefault = customers: CustomerType.t => {
  id: Belt.Array.length(customers) + 1,
  name: "",
  address: {
    street: "",
    city: "",
    state: "",
    zip: "",
  },
  phone: "",
  email: "",
};
```

And, of course, the following is our component's `make` function:

```
let make = _children => {
  ...component,
  initialState: () => {
    let mode = Js.String.includes("create", pathname) ? Create : Update;
    {
      mode,
      customer:
        switch (mode) {
        | Create => getDefault(customers)
        | Update =>
          Belt.Option.getWithDefault(
            getCustomer(customers),
            getDefault(customers),
          )
        },
    };
  },
  reducer: (action, state) =>
    switch (action) {
    | Save(event) =>
      ReactEvent.Form.preventDefault(event);
      ReasonReact.Update(state);
    },
  render: self =>
    <form
      className=Styles.form
      onSubmit={
        event => {
          ReactEvent.Form.persist(event);
```

[135]

JSON in Reason

```
              self.send(Save(event));
            }
          }>
          <label>
            {ReasonReact.string("Name")}
            <input type_="text" defaultValue={self.state.customer.name} />
          </label>
          <label>
            {ReasonReact.string("Street Address")}
            <input
              type_="text"
              defaultValue={self.state.customer.address.street}
            />
          </label>
          <label>
            {ReasonReact.string("City")}
            <input type_="text" defaultValue={self.state.customer.address.city}
 />
          </label>
          <label>
            {ReasonReact.string("State")}
            <input type_="text"
  defaultValue={self.state.customer.address.state} />
          </label>
          <label>
            {ReasonReact.string("Zip")}
            <input type_="text" defaultValue={self.state.customer.address.zip}
 />
          </label>
          <label>
            {ReasonReact.string("Phone")}
            <input type_="text" defaultValue={self.state.customer.phone} />
          </label>
          <label>
            {ReasonReact.string("Email")}
            <input type_="text" defaultValue={self.state.customer.email} />
          </label>
          <input
            type_="submit"
            value={
              switch (self.state.mode) {
              | Create => "Create"
              | Update => "Update"
              }
            }
          />
        </form>,
    };
```

The `Save` action doesn't yet save to `localStorage`. The form is empty when navigating to `/customers/create` and populated when navigating to, for example, `/customers/1`.

Integrating with localStorage

Let's create a separate module to interact with the data layer, which we'll call `DataPureReason.re`. Here, we expose bindings to `localStorage.getItem` and `localStorage.setItem`, and a parsing function to parse JSON strings into the `CustomerType.t` record defined earlier.

Populating localStorage

You'll find some initial data in `Chapter07/app-end/src/customers/data.json`. Please run `localStorage.setItem("customers", JSON.stringify(/* paste JSON data here */))` in your browser's console to populate `localStorage` with this initial data.

DataPureReason.re

Remember when BuckleScript bindings felt kind of obscure? Hopefully, they're now starting to feel a bit more straightforward:

```
[@bs.val] [@bs.scope "localStorage"] external getItem: string => string = "";
[@bs.val] [@bs.scope "localStorage"]
external setItem: (string, string) => unit = "";
```

To parse the JSON, we'll use the `Js.Json` module.

> The Js.Json documentation can be found at the following URL:
>
> https://bucklescript.github.io/bucklescript/api/Js_json.html

Soon, you'll see one way to use the `Js.Json` module to parse JSON strings. One caveat, though: it's a bit tedious. But it's important to understand what is going on and why we need to do this for typed languages such as Reason. At a high level, we will validate the JSON string to ensure that it's valid JSON, and if so use the `Js.Json.classify` function to convert the JSON string (`Js.Json.t`) into a tagged type (`Js.Json.tagged_t`). The available tags are as follows:

```
type tagged_t =
  | JSONFalse
  | JSONTrue
  | JSONNull
  | JSONString(string)
  | JSONNumber(float)
  | JSONObject(Js_dict.t(t))
  | JSONArray(array(t));
```

This way, we can convert JSON strings into typed Reason data structures.

Validating JSON strings

The `getItem` binding defined in the previous section will return a string:

```
let unvalidated = DataPureReason.getItem("customers");
```

We can validate the JSON string like so:

```
let validated =
  try (Js.Json.parseExn(unvalidated)) {
  | _ => failwith("Error parsing JSON string")
  };
```

If the JSON is not valid, it will generate a runtime error. At the end of the chapter, we'll learn how GraphQL can help improve this situation.

Using Js.Json.classify

Let's assume that we've validated the following JSON (it's an array of objects):

```
[
  {
    "id": 1,
    "name": "Christina Langworth",
    "address": {
      "street": "81 Casey Stravenue",
      "city": "Beattyview",
```

```
            "state": "TX",
            "zip": "57918"
        },
        "phone": "877-549-1362",
        "email": "Christina.Langworth@gmail.com"
    },
    {
        "id": 2,
        "name": "Victor Tillman",
        "address": {
            "street": "2811 Toby Gardens",
            "city": "West Enrique",
            "state": "NV",
            "zip": "40465"
        },
        "phone": "(502) 091-2292",
        "email": "Victor.Tillman30@gmail.com"
    }
]
```

Now that we have validated the JSON, we're ready to classify it:

```
switch (Js.Json.classify(validated)) {
| Js.Json.JSONArray(array) =>
  Belt.Array.map(array, customer => ...)
| _ => failwith("Expected an array")
};
```

We pattern-match on the possible tags for `Js.Json.tagged_t`. If it's an array, we then map over it using `Belt.Array.map` (or `Js.Array.map`). Otherwise, we get a runtime error in the context of our application.

The `map` function is passed a reference to each object in the array. But Reason doesn't yet know that each element is an object. Inside the `map`, we once again classify each element of the array. After classifying, Reason now knows that each element is, in fact, an object. We'll define a custom helper function called `parseCustomer` for use with the `map` function:

```
switch (Js.Json.classify(validated)) {
| Js.Json.JSONArray(array) =>
  Belt.Array.map(array, customer => parseCustomer(customer))
| _ => failwith("Expected an array")
};

let parseCustomer = json =>
  switch (Js.Json.classify(json)) {
  | Js.Json.JSONObject(json) => (
      ...
```

[139]

JSON in Reason

```
    )
    | _ => failwith("Expected an object")
    };
```

Now, if each element of the array is an object, we want to return a new record. This record will be of type `CustomerType.t`. Otherwise, we get a runtime error:

```
let parseCustomer = json =>
  switch (Js.Json.classify(json)) {
  | Js.Json.JSONObject(json) => (
      {
        id: ...,
        name: ...,
        address: ...,
        phone: ...,
        email: ...,
      }: CustomerType.t
    )
  | _ => failwith("Expected an object")
  };
```

Now, for each field (that is, `id`, `name`, `address`, and so on), we use `Js.Dict.get` to get and classify each field:

> The `Js.Dict` documentation can be found at the following URL:
>
> https://bucklescript.github.io/bucklescript/api/Js.Dict.html

```
let parseCustomer = json =>
  switch (Js.Json.classify(json)) {
  | Js.Json.JSONObject(json) => (
      {
        id:
          switch (Js.Dict.get(json, "id")) {
          | Some(id) =>
            switch (Js.Json.classify(id)) {
            | Js.Json.JSONNumber(id) => int_of_float(id)
            | _ => failwith("Field 'id' should be a number")
            }
          | None => failwith("Missing field: id")
          },
        name:
          switch (Js.Dict.get(json, "name")) {
          | Some(name) =>
            switch (Js.Json.classify(name)) {
            | Js.Json.JSONString(name) => name
```

```
            | _ => failwith("Field 'name' should be a string")
            }
          | None => failwith("Missing field: name")
          },
        address:
          switch (Js.Dict.get(json, "address")) {
          | Some(address) =>
            switch (Js.Json.classify(address)) {
            | Js.Json.JSONObject(address) => {
                street:
                  switch (Js.Dict.get(address, "street")) {
                  | Some(street) =>
                    switch (Js.Json.classify(street)) {
                    | Js.Json.JSONString(street) => street
                    | _ => failwith("Field 'street' should be a string")
                    }
                  | None => failwith("Missing field: street")
                  },
                city: ...,
                state: ...,
                zip: ...,
              }
            | _ => failwith("Field 'address' should be a object")
            }
          | None => failwith("Missing field: address")
          },
        phone: ...,
        email: ...,
      }: CustomerType.t
    )
  | _ => failwith("Expected an object")
  };
```

> See `src/customers/DataPureReason.re` for the full implementation. `DataPureReason.rei` hides implementation details and only exposes the `localStorage` bindings and a parse function.

Phew, that was a bit tedious, wasn't it? Now that it's done though, we can replace the hardcoded customer array in both `CustomerList.re` and `Customer.re` with the following:

```
let customers =
  DataBsJson.(parse(getItem("customers")));
```

So far, so good! The JSON data is being pulled in dynamically, and parsed, and now works the same as it did when hardcoded.

JSON in Reason

Writing to localStorage

Let's now add the functionality to create and update customers. To do this, we'll need to convert our Reason data structure to JSON. In the interface file, `DataPureReason.rei`, we'll expose a `toJson` function:

```
/* DataPureReason.rei */
let parse: string => array(CustomerType.t);
let toJson: array(CustomerType.t) => string;
```

And then we'll implement it:

```
/* DataPureReason.re */
let customerToJson = (customer: CustomerType.t) => {
  let id = customer.id;
  let name = customer.name;
  let street = customer.address.street;
  let city = customer.address.city;
  let state = customer.address.state;
  let zip = customer.address.zip;
  let phone = customer.phone;
  let email = customer.email;

  {j|
    {
      "id": $id,
      "name": "$name",
      "address": {
        "street": "$street",
        "city": "$city",
        "state": "$state",
        "zip": "$zip"
      },
      "phone": "$phone",
      "email": "$email"
    }
  |j};
};

let toJson = (customers: array(CustomerType.t)) =>
  Belt.Array.map(customers, customer => customerToJson(customer))
  ->Belt.Array.reduce("[", (acc, customer) => acc ++ customer ++ ",")
  ->Js.String.replaceByRe([%bs.re "/,$/"], "", _)
  ++ "]"
    ->Js.String.split("/n", _)
    ->Js.Array.map(line => Js.String.trim(line), _)
    ->Js.Array.joinWith("", _);
```

[142]

Chapter 7

And then we'll use the `toJson` function in the `Customer.re` reducer:

```
reducer: (action, state) =>
  switch (action) {
  | Save(event) =>
    let getInputValue: string => string = [%raw
      (selector => "return document.querySelector(selector).value")
    ];
    ReactEvent.Form.preventDefault(event);
    ReasonReact.UpdateWithSideEffects(
      {
        ...state,
        customer: {
          id: state.customer.id,
          name: getInputValue("input[name=name]"),
          address: {
            street: getInputValue("input[name=street]"),
            city: getInputValue("input[name=city]"),
            state: getInputValue("input[name=state]"),
            zip: getInputValue("input[name=zip]"),
          },
          phone: getInputValue("input[name=phone]"),
          email: getInputValue("input[name=email]"),
        },
      },
      (
        self => {
          let customers =
            switch (self.state.mode) {
            | Create =>
              Belt.Array.concat(customers, [|self.state.customer|])
            | Update =>
              Belt.Array.setExn(
                customers,
                Js.Array.findIndex(
                  customer =>
                    customer.CustomerType.id == self.state.customer.id,
                  customers,
                ),
                self.state.customer,
              );
              customers;
            };

          let json = customers->DataPureReason.toJson;
          DataPureReason.setItem("customers", json);
        }
      ),
```

[143]

JSON in Reason

```
    );
},
```

In the reducer, we update `self.state.customer` with values from the DOM, and then call a function that updates `localStorage`. Now, we're able to write to `localStorage` by creating or updating customers. Navigate to `/customers/create` to create a new customer, and then navigate back to `/customers` to see your newly added customer. Click on a customer to navigate to the update view, update the customer, click the **Update** button, and refresh the page.

Using bs-json

Now that we understand exactly how to convert JSON strings into typed Reason data structures, we notice that the process is a bit tedious. It's more lines of code than one would expect coming from a dynamic language such as JavaScript. Also, there is quite a bit of repetitive code. As an alternative, many in the Reason community have adopted `bs-json` as an "official" solution for encoding and decoding JSON.

Let's create a new module called `DataBsJson.re` and a new interface file, `DataBsJson.rei`. We'll copy the exact same interface as we had in `DataPureReason.rei` so that we know that, once we're done, we'll be able to replace all references to `DataPureReason` with `DataBsJson` and everything should work the same.

The exposed interface is as follows:

```
/* DataBsJson.rei */
[@bs.val] [@bs.scope "localStorage"] external getItem: string => string = "";
[@bs.val] [@bs.scope "localStorage"]
external setItem: (string, string) => unit = "";

let parse: string => array(CustomerType.t);
let toJson: array(CustomerType.t) => string;
```

Let's focus on the `parse` function:

```
let parse = json =>
  json |> Json.parseOrRaise |> Json.Decode.array(customerDecoder);
```

Chapter 7

Here, we are accepting the same JSON string as before, validating it, converting it to a `Js.Json.t` (via `Json.parseOrRaise`), and then passing the result into this new `Json.Decode.array(customerDecoder)` function. `Json.Decode.array` will attempt to decode the JSON string into an array, and decode each element of the array with a custom function called `customerDecoder`—which we'll see next:

```
let customerDecoder = json =>
  Json.Decode.(
    (
      {
        id: json |> field("id", int),
        name: json |> field("name", string),
        address: json |> field("address", addressDecoder),
        phone: json |> field("phone", string),
        email: json |> field("email", string),
      }: CustomerType.t
    )
  );
```

The `customerDecoder` function accepts the JSON associated with each element of the array and tries to decode that into a record of type `CustomerType.t`. This is pretty much exactly the same as what we did previously, but it's much less verbose and much easier to read. As you can see, we have another customer decoder, called `addressDecoder`, which is used to decode the `CustomerType.address` type:

```
let addressDecoder = json =>
  Json.Decode.(
    (
      {
        street: json |> field("street", string),
        city: json |> field("city", string),
        state: json |> field("state", string),
        zip: json |> field("zip", string),
      }: CustomerType.address
    )
  );
```

Notice how the custom decoders are easily composed. Each record field is decoded by calling `Json.Decode.field`, passing the name of the field (on the JSON side), and passing in a `Json.Decode` function that ultimately converts the JSON field to a type Reason can understand.

JSON in Reason

Encoding works similarly, but in the reverse order:

```
let toJson = (customers: array(CustomerType.t)) =>
  customers->Belt.Array.map(customer =>
    Json.Encode.(
      object_([
        ("id", int(customer.id)),
        ("name", string(customer.name)),
        (
          "address",
          object_([
            ("street", string(customer.address.street)),
            ("city", string(customer.address.city)),
            ("state", string(customer.address.state)),
            ("zip", string(customer.address.zip)),
          ]),
        ),
        ("phone", string(customer.phone)),
        ("email", string(customer.email)),
      ])
    )
  )
  |> Json.Encode.jsonArray
  |> Json.stringify;
```

The array of customers is mapped and each customer is encoded to a JSON object. The result is an array of JSON objects, which then gets encoded to JSON, and stringified. Much better than our previous implementation.

After copying over the same `localStorage` bindings from `DataPureReason.re`, our interface is now implemented. After replacing all references to `DataPureReason` with `DataBsJson`, we see that our app is working just the same.

Using GraphQL

At ReactiveConf 2018, there was an amazing talk by Sean Grove on Reason and GraphQL titled *ReactiveMeetups w/ Sean Grove | ReasonML GraphQL*. The following is an excerpt from this talk that nicely summarizes the problems and solution for using JSON in Reason:

> So I would argue that, in typed languages, like Reason, there are three really, really big problems when you want to interact with the real world.

The first is all the boilerplate that it takes to get data into and out of your type system. The second is, even if you can program your way out of the boilerplate, you are still worried about the accuracy, the safety of conversion.
And then finally, even if you if you get all of this and you're absolutely sure you've caught all the variation, someone can still change it from underneath you without you knowing.

How many times do we get a changelog whenever the server changes fields? In an ideal world, we would. But most of the time we don't. We get to reverse-engineer what our server changed.

So I would argue that, in order to solve this in a broadly applicable way, we want four things:

1) Access to all of the data types that an API can provide to us in a programmatic way.
2) Automatic conversions that are guaranteed to be safe.
3) And we want to have a contract. We want the server to guarantee if it said a field is not nullable, they will never give us null. If they change the field name, then we immediately know and that they know.
4) And we want all of that in a programmatic way.

And that's GraphQL.

-Sean Grove

> You can find the video of *ReactiveMeetups w/ Sean Grove | ReasonML GraphQL* at the following URL:
> `https://youtu.be/t9a-_VnNilE`
>
> And, here is ReactiveConf's Youtube channel:
> `https://www.youtube.com/channel/UCBHdUnixTWymmXBIw12Y8Qg`

It's beyond the scope of this book to go too deeply into GraphQL, but a high-level introduction seems fitting given that we're discussing using JSON in Reason.

What is GraphQL?

If you're part of the ReactJS community, then you've likely already heard of GraphQL. GraphQL is a query language and a runtime we can use to fulfill those queries and was also created by Facebook. With GraphQL, ReactJS components can include GraphQL fragments for data that a component requires—this means that a component can couple HTML, CSS, JavaScript, and its external data all in one file.

When using GraphQL, do I need to create JSON decoders?

Since GraphQL knows your application's external data intimately, the GraphQL client (`reason-apollo`) will generate the decoders for you automatically. Of course, the decoders would have to be automatically generated so we're confident that they reflect the current shape of the external data. This is just another reason to consider using GraphQL with your Reason application when you need to handle external data.

Summary

As long as we're working within Reason, the type system will prevent you from running into runtime type errors. However, when interacting with the outside world—whether it be JavaScript or external data—we lose those guarantees. To be able to preserve these guarantees within Reason's boundaries, we need to help out the type system when using things outside Reason. We previously learned how to use external JavaScript in Reason, and in this chapter we've learned how to use external data in Reason. Although writing decoders and encoders is more challenging, it's quite similar to writing JavaScript bindings. In the end, we're simply telling Reason the type of something external to Reason. With GraphQL, we can extend the boundaries of Reason to include external data. There are trade-offs, and nothing is perfect, but it's definitely worth giving GraphQL a shot.

In the next chapter, we'll explore testing in the context of Reason. What tests should we write? What tests should we avoid? We'll also explore how unit testing can help us improve the code we wrote in this chapter.

8
Unit Testing in Reason

The subject of testing in a typed language such as Reason is a somewhat controversial topic. Some believe that a good test suite diminishes the need for a type system. On the other hand, some value a type system much more than their test suite. These differences in opinion can lead to some pretty heated debates.

Of course, types and tests are not mutually exclusive. We can have types *and* tests. Perhaps Cheng Lou, one of Reason's core team members, said it best.

> *Tests. That's an easy one, right? Types kill a category of tests—not all of the tests. And this is a discussion that people don't appreciate enough. They all pit tests against types. The point is: if you have types, and you add tests, your tests will be able to express much more with less energy. You don't need to assert on invalid input anymore. You can assert on something more important. Tests can be there if you want; you're just saying much more with them.*
>
> *- Cheng Lou*

You can watch Cheng Lou's talk at React Conf 2017 on the following URL: `https://youtu.be/_0T50SSzxms`

In this chapter, we'll set up Jest, the popular JavaScript testing framework, via the `bs-jest` BuckleScript bindings. We will do the following:

- Learn how to set up `bs-jest` with both the `es6` and `commonjs` module formats
- Unit-test a Reason function
- See how writing tests can help us improve our code

Unit Testing in Reason

To follow along, clone this book's GitHub repository and start from `Chapter08/app-start` using the following code:

```
git clone https://github.com/PacktPublishing/ReasonML-Quick-Start-Guide.git
cd ReasonML-Quick-Start-Guide
cd Chapter08/app-start
npm install
```

Testing with Jest

Jest, also created by Facebook, is arguably one of the most popular JavaScript testing frameworks. If you're familiar with React, you're likely also familiar with Jest. Therefore, we'll skip the formal introduction and get started with using Jest in Reason.

Installation

Just like any other package, we start with the **Reason Package Index** (or **Redex**, for short).

> Reason Package Index:
>
> https://redex.github.io/

Typing in `jest` reveals the `bs-jest` bindings to Jest. Following the installation instructions for `bs-jest`, we first install `bs-jest` with npm:

```
npm install --save-dev @glennsl/bs-jest
```

Then we let BuckleScript know about this dev dependency by including it in `bsconfig.json`. Notice that the key is `"bs-dev-dependencies"` and not `"bs-dependencies"`:

```
"bs-dev-dependencies": ["@glennsl/bs-jest"]
```

Since `bs-jest` lists `jest` as a dependency, npm will install `jest` as well, and we don't need to include `jest` as a direct dependency of our application.

Let's now create a `__tests__` directory as a sibling of the `src` directory:

```
cd Chapter08/app-start
mkdir __tests__
```

And tell BuckleScript to look for this directory:

```
/* bsconfig.json */
...
"sources": [
  {
    "dir": "src",
    "subdirs": true
  },
  {
    "dir": "__tests__",
    "type": "dev"
  }
],
...
```

Lastly, we'll update our `test` script in `package.json` to use Jest:

```
/* package.json */
"test": "jest"
```

Our first test

Let's create our first test in `__tests__/First_test.re` with something simple for now:

```
/* __tests__/First_test.re */
open Jest;

describe("Expect", () =>
  Expect.(test("toBe", () =>
          expect(1 + 2) |> toBe(3)
        ))
);
```

Running `npm test` now fails with the following error:

```
FAIL lib/es6/__tests__/First_test.bs.js
  ● Test suite failed to run

    Jest encountered an unexpected token

    This usually means that you are trying to import a file which Jest
    cannot parse, e.g. it's not plain JavaScript.

    By default, if Jest sees a Babel config, it will use that to transform
    your files, ignoring "node_modules".
```

[151]

```
Here's what you can do:
 • To have some of your "node_modules" files transformed, you can
   specify a custom "transformIgnorePatterns" in your config.
 • If you need a custom transformation specify a "transform" option in
   your config.
 • If you simply want to mock your non-JS modules (e.g. binary assets)
   you can stub them out with the "moduleNameMapper" config option.

You'll find more details and examples of these config options in the
docs:
https://jestjs.io/docs/en/configuration.html

Details:

.../lib/es6/__tests__/First_test.bs.js:3
import * as Jest from "@glennsl/bs-jest/lib/es6/src/jest.js";
       ^

SyntaxError: Unexpected token *

    at ScriptTransformer._transformAndBuildScript (node_modules/jest-
    runtime/build/script_transformer.js:403:17)

Test Suites: 1 failed, 1 total
Tests:       0 total
Snapshots:   0 total
Time:        1.43s
Ran all test suites.
npm ERR! Test failed. See above for more details.
```

The problem here is that Jest cannot directly understand the ES Module format. Remember that we've configured BuckleScript to use ES modules via the following configuration (see Chapter 2, *Setting Up a Development Environment*):

```
/* bsconfig.json */
...
"package-specs": [
  {
    "module": "es6"
  }
],
...
```

One way to resolve this issue is to configure BuckleScript to use the `"commonjs"` module format instead:

```
/* bsconfig.json */
...
"package-specs": [
  {
    "module": "commonjs"
  }
],
...
```

We'll then also need to update webpack's `entry` field:

```
/* webpack.config.js */
...
entry: "./lib/js/src/Index.bs.js", /* changed es6 to js */
...
```

Now, running `npm test` results in a test that passes:

```
PASS lib/js/__tests__/First_test.bs.js
  Expect
    ✓ toBe (4ms)

Test Suites: 1 passed, 1 total
Tests: 1 passed, 1 total
Snapshots: 0 total
Time: 1.322s
Ran all test suites.
```

Alternatively, if we want to keep using the ES module format, we need to make sure Jest runs the `*test.bs.js` files through Babel first. To do this, we'll need to follow the following steps:

1. Install both `babel-jest` and `babel-preset-env`:

   npm install babel-core@6.26.3 babel-jest@23.6.0 babel-preset-env@1.7.0

2. Add the corresponding Babel configuration in `.babelrc`:

   ```
   /* .babelrc */
   {
     "presets": ["env"]
   }
   ```

[153]

Unit Testing in Reason

3. Ensure that Jest runs certain third-party dependencies within `node_modules` through Babel. Jest excludes running anything in `node_modules` through Babel by default for performance reasons. We can override this behavior by providing a custom Jest configuration in `package.json`. Here, we'll tell Jest to only ignore third-party dependencies that don't match `/node_modules/glennsl*`, `/node_modules/bs-platform*`, and so on:

```
/* package.json */
...
"jest": {
  "transformIgnorePatterns": [
    "/node_modules/(?!@glennsl|bs-platform|bs-css|reason-react)"
  ]
}
```

Now, running `npm test` works with the ES Module format:

```
PASS lib/es6/__tests__/First_test.bs.js
  Expect
    ✓ toBe (7ms)

Test Suites: 1 passed, 1 total
Tests: 1 passed, 1 total
Snapshots: 0 total
Time: 1.041s
Ran all test suites.
```

Testing business logic

Let's write a test that verifies we're able to get the right customer by its `id`. In `Customer.re`, there is a function called `getCustomer` that accepts an array of `customers`, and imperatively gets the `id` by calling `getId`. The `getId` function accepts a `pathname` that exists outside the scope of `getCustomer`:

```
let getCustomer = customers => {
  let id = getId(pathname);
  customers |> Js.Array.find(customer => customer.CustomerType.id == id);
};
```

Right away, we notice that this is less than ideal. It would be much better if `getCustomer` accepted an array of `customers` *and* an `id`, and focused on getting the customer by their `id`. Otherwise, it will be harder to write a test *just* for `getCustomer`.

So, we refactor `getCustomer` to also accept an `id`:

```
let getCustomerById = (customers, id) => {
  customers |> Js.Array.find(customer => customer.CustomerType.id == id);
};
```

Now, we can more easily write the test. Follow the compiler errors to ensure that you've replaced `getCustomer` with `getCustomerById`. For the `id` argument, pass in `getId(pathname)`.

Let's rename our test to `__tests__/Customers_test.re` and include the following test:

```
open Jest;

describe("Customer", () =>
  Expect.(
    test("can create a customer", () => {
      let customers: array(CustomerType.t) = [|
        {
          id: 1,
          name: "Irita Camsey",
          address: {
            street: "69 Ryan Parkway",
            city: "Kansas City",
            state: "MO",
            zip: "00494",
          },
          phone: "8169271752",
          email: "icamsey0@over-blog.com",
        },
        {
          id: 2,
          name: "Luise Grayson",
          address: {
            street: "2756 Gale Trail",
            city: "Jacksonville",
            state: "FL",
            zip: "23566",
          },
          phone: "9044985243",
          email: "lgrayson1@netlog.com",
        },
        {
          id: 3,
          name: "Derick Whitelaw",
          address: {
            street: "45 Southridge Par",
            city: "Lexington",
```

Unit Testing in Reason

```
              state: "KY",
              zip: "08037",
            },
            phone: "4079634850",
            email: "dwhitelaw2@fema.gov",
          },
        |];
        let customer: CustomerType.t =
          Customer.getCustomerById(customers, 2) |> Belt.Option.getExn;
        expect((customer.id, customer.name)) |> toEqual((2, "Luise
          Grayson"));
      })
    )
  );
```

Running this test (via `npm test`) with our existing code results in the following error:

```
FAIL lib/es6/__tests__/Customers_test.bs.js
  ● Test suite failed to run

    Error: No message was provided

Test Suites: 1 failed, 1 total
Tests: 0 total
Snapshots: 0 total
Time: 1.711s
Ran all test suites.
```

The reason for the error is that `Customers.re` makes a call to `localStorage` at the top level.

```
/* Customer.re */
let customers = DataBsJson.(parse(getItem("customers"))); /* this is the problem */
```

Since Jest runs in Node.js, we don't have access to browser APIs. To resolve this issue, we can wrap this call in a function:

```
/* Customer.re */
let getCustomers = () => DataBsJson.(parse(getItem("customers")));
```

And we can call this `getCustomers` function within `initialState`. This will allow us to avoid the call to `localStorage` from within Jest.

Let's update `Customer.re` to move the array of customers into the state:

```
/* Customer.re */
...
type state = {
  mode,
  customer: CustomerType.t,
  customers: array(CustomerType.t),
};

...

let getCustomers = () => DataBsJson.(parse(getItem("customers")));

let getCustomerById = (customers, id) => {
  customers |> Js.Array.find(customer => customer.CustomerType.id == id);
};

...

initialState: () => {
  let mode = Js.String.includes("create", pathname) ? Create : Update;
  let customers = getCustomers();
  {
    mode,
    customer:
      switch (mode) {
      | Create => getDefault(customers)
      | Update =>
        Belt.Option.getWithDefault(
          getCustomerById(customers, getId(pathname)),
          getDefault(customers),
        )
      },
    customers,
  };
},

...

/* within the reducer */
ReasonReact.UpdateWithSideEffects(
  {
    ...state,
    customer: {
      id: state.customer.id,
      name: getInputValue("input[name=name]"),
      address: {
```

```
              street: getInputValue("input[name=street]"),
              city: getInputValue("input[name=city]"),
              state: getInputValue("input[name=state]"),
              zip: getInputValue("input[name=zip]"),
            },
            phone: getInputValue("input[name=phone]"),
            email: getInputValue("input[name=email]"),
          },
        },
        self => {
          let customers =
            switch (self.state.mode) {
            | Create =>
              Belt.Array.concat(state.customers, [|self.state.customer|])
            | Update =>
              Belt.Array.setExn(
                state.customers,
                Js.Array.findIndex(
                  customer =>
                    customer.CustomerType.id == self.state.customer.id,
                  state.customers,
                ),
                self.state.customer,
              );
              state.customers;
            };

          let json = customers->DataBsJson.toJson;
          DataBsJson.setItem("customers", json);
        },
      );
```

After these changes, our test succeeds:

```
 PASS lib/es6/__tests__/Customers_test.bs.js
  Customer
    ✓ can create a customer (5ms)

Test Suites: 1 passed, 1 total
Tests: 1 passed, 1 total
Snapshots: 0 total
Time: 1.179s
Ran all test suites.
```

Reflecting

In this chapter, we learned the basics of setting up `bs-jest` with both the CommonJS and ES Module formats. We also learned that unit testing can help force us to write better code because, for the most part, code that is easier to test is also better. We refactored `getCustomer` to `getCustomerById`, and moved the array of customers into that component's state.

Since we've written our unit tests in Reason, the compiler checks our tests as well. For example, if `Customer_test.re` uses `getCustomer` and we change `getCustomerById` to `getCustomer` in `Customer.re`, we get a compile time error:

```
We've found a bug for you!
/__tests__/Customers_test.re 45:9-28

43  |];
44  let customer: CustomerType.t =
45    Customer.getCustomer(customers, 2) |> Belt.Option.getExn;
46    expect((customer.id, customer.name)) |> toEqual((2, "Luise Grayson"))
      );
47  })

The value getCustomer can't be found in Customer

Hint: Did you mean getCustomers?
```

This means that we're also not able to write certain unit tests. For example, if we wanted to test `Chapter 5`, *Effective ML* codes, where we used the type system to guarantee that an invoice wouldn't be discounted twice, the test wouldn't even compile. How lovely.

Summary

Since Reason's reach is so broad, there are so many different ways to approach learning it. This book has focused on learning Reason from the perspective of a frontend developer. We've taken skills and concepts that we're already familiar with (such as building web applications with ReactJS) and explored how we would do the same with Reason. While on this journey, we learned about Reason's type system, its toolchain, and its ecosystem.

I believe the future of Reason is bright. Many of the skills we've learned are directly transferable to targeting a native platform. Reason's frontend story is currently more polished than its native story, but it's already possible to compile to both web and native. And it's only going to get better from here. There have already been huge improvements from when I first started using Reason, and I'm so excited to see what the future holds.

Hopefully this book has piqued your interest in Reason, OCaml, and the ML family of languages in general. Reason's type system has seen decades of engineering. As a result, there is a lot that this book hasn't covered, and I'm still learning myself. However, you should by now have a solid foundation on which to continue your learning. I encourage you to learn publicly by writing asking questions on the Discord channel, writing blog posts, mentoring others, sharing your journey in meetups, and so on.

Thank you very much for making it this far, and see you on the Discord channel!

Reason Discord channel:

```
https://discord.gg/reasonml
```

Other Books You May Enjoy

If you enjoyed this book, you may be interested in these other books by Packt:

Learn Type-Driven Development
Yawar Amin, Kamon Ayeva

ISBN: 9781788838016

- Use static types to capture information, making programs safer and faster
- Learn ReasonML from experienced type-driven developers
- Enhance safety by simply using basic types
- Understand the most important type-driven concepts with simple examples
- Explore a design space using static typing and find the best way to express your system rules
- Use static types and dynamic runtime in harmony to write even safer and faster code

Hands-On Functional Programming with TypeScript
Remo H. Jansen

ISBN: 9781788831437

- Understand the pros and cons of functional programming
- Delve into the principles, patterns, and best practices of functional and reactive programming
- Use lazy evaluation to improve the performance of applications
- Explore functional optics with Ramda
- Gain insights into category theory functional data structures such as Functors and Monads
- Use functions as values, so that they can be passed as arguments to other functions

Leave a review - let other readers know what you think

Please share your thoughts on this book with others by leaving a review on the site that you bought it from. If you purchased the book from Amazon, please leave us an honest review on this book's Amazon page. This is vital so that other potential readers can see and use your unbiased opinion to make purchasing decisions, we can understand what our customers think about our products, and our authors can see your feedback on the title that they have worked with Packt to create. It will only take a few minutes of your time, but is valuable to other potential customers, our authors, and Packt. Thank you!

Index

A
abstract type 69
action 50
advanced type system
 features 114
arrays 77, 78

B
Belt standard library
 using 79
Belt
 currying 89, 90
 List module 86
 Option module 85, 86
 uncurried functions 90, 91
 using 85
bs-css
 using 122, 124, 125
bs-json
 using 144, 145
bsconfig.json file
 about 29, 30
 package-specs field 31
 reference 32
 sources field 32
 structure 130
 suffix field 32
 warnings field 31
BuckleScript documentation
 reference 95
BuckleScript
 [@bs.deriving abstract] 97, 98
 built-in JavaScript bindings 79
 installing 26
 references 8

C
children prop 45
client-side routing
 about 68, 69
 current route 70, 71
 helper functions 71, 72
 usage 73
component creation, basics
 about 40
 children 45, 47
 component templates 41
 event handlers 42
 JSX 43, 44
 life cycles 47, 48
 props 44
 self 42
 subscriptions helper 48
 unit 42, 43
component templates 41
CSS-in-JS Reason libraries 126
CSS-in-JS
 about 117
 history 118
 trade-offs 126
currying 89, 90
custom bindings
 using 79
Customer.re file 133, 134, 135
CustomerList.re file 132
CustomerType.re file 131

D
data structures
 about 77
 arrays 77, 78
 lists 81, 82

DataPureReason.re
  about 137
  Js.Json.classify, using 138, 139, 141
  JSON strings, validating 138
decorators
  [@bs.module] decorator 94
  [@bs.scope] decorator 93
  [@bs.send] decorator 93
  [@bs.val] decorator 92
DOM, in pure Reason 32, 33, 34

E

ES Module (ESM) 33
event handler 42

G

generalized algebraic datatypes (GADTs) 114
GraphQL
  about 147
  using 146
Gravitron
  reference 11

I

instance variables
  about 55
  mutable records 55
  ref 55, 56

J

JavaScript
  interoperability 92
  using, in Reason 92
Jest
  testing with 150
Js.Dict documentation
  reference 140
Js.Json documentation
  reference 137
Js.t Object 61
JSX 43, 44

L

labelled arguments 44
life cycle events 47, 48
List module, Belt
  deck of cards example 88
  make function 86
  makeBy function 87
  reference 86
  shuffle function 87
  take function 87
lists
  about 81, 82
  recursion 82, 83, 84
localStorage
  integrating with 137
  populating 137
  writing to 142, 143, 144

M

module scope 75, 77
module signature
  about 102
  abstract types 103, 104
  module types 103
  using 104, 105, 107, 109
mutable records 55

N

navigation menu
  about 57, 59
  actions, adding 61, 63
  bindings 59, 60
  events 60
  inline styles 64, 65
  Js.t Object 61
  React ref 66
  updating 131
  velocity 66, 67, 68
normal variants 114

O

OCaml 7
Option module, Belt 86
  about 85

reference 86

P

pattern matching
  reference 12
phantom types 109, 110, 111
pipe operators
  about 84, 85
  reference 12
polymorphic type 21
polymorphic variant 95
polymorphic variants 112, 113
props 44
pure Reason project
  bsconfig.json file 29, 30
  DOM 32, 33, 34
  setting up 27, 28

R

raw JavaScript
  using 80
React ref 66
React Transition Group documentation
  reference 96
ReactJS components
  binding to 96
  dependencies, importing 96
  make functions, creating 97
  using 98, 99
Reason Discord channel
  reference 115
Reason editor support documentation
  reference 26
Reason Package Index
  reference 150
Reason standard library
  using 78
Reason toolchain
  about 26
  BuckleScript 26
  editor configuration 26
Reason
  about 7
  community 13
  cross-platform 11
  data structures 16
  ES2030 12
  exploring 14, 15
  immutability support 8, 9, 10
  interoperability 12
  invalid states 23
  JavaScript, using in 92
  maintainability 12
  module system 11
  need for 8
  pattern matching 17, 18, 19, 20, 21
  purity 9, 10
  reference 7
  type system 11
Reasonable APIs 94, 95
ReasonML 7
ReasonReact 13
ReasonReact project
  developer experience, improving 35, 36
  setting up 34, 35
Redex (Reason Package Index)
  reference 126
reducer 50
ref 56
router
  updating 130

S

self argument 42
singly linked lists 82
state 50
stateful components
  action 50
  creating 48
  instance variables 55
  reducer 50
  refactoring 51, 52, 54
  state 49, 50
styled-components
  [@bs.variadic] 120, 121
  using 118, 119, 120
subscriptions helper 48
synthetic events
  reference 61

T

testing, with Jest
  about 150
  business logic 154, 156, 158
  first test, creating 151, 152, 154
  installation 150, 151
type variables 21, 78

U

uncurried functions
  about 90, 91
  makeByU 91
unit type 42, 43

V

views
  building 130
VSCode
  configuring 26

CPSIA information can be obtained
at www.ICGtesting.com
Printed in the USA
FFHW012049070419
51592073-57018FF